Communication Counts

Speech and Language Difficulties in the Early Years

Fleur Griffiths
and collaborators

David Fulton Publishers
London

David Fulton Publishers Ltd
The Chiswick Centre, 414 Chiswick High Road, London W4 5TF

www.fultonpublishers.co.uk

First published in Great Britain in 2002 by David Fulton Publishers

British Library Cataloguing in Publication Data
A catalogue record for this book is available from the British Library.

ISBN 1 85346 797 9

Typeset by Servis Filmsetting Ltd, Manchester
Printed and bound in Great Britain by The Cromwell Press, Trowbridge, Wilts.

Contents

Like bread and love, language is for sharing.
(Carlos Fuentes)

I am certain of nothing but the holiness of the heart's affections and the
truth of imagination.
(Keats, letter to Benjamin Bailey, 1817)

Acknowledgements

This book has emerged, thanks to my collaborators and colleagues; the children and their parents, especially Jon and Stephen Laws; supportive work contexts at Sunderland University, School of Education, at North Tyneside and Sunderland Local Education Authorities, at the national charity, I CAN; and the help of particular individuals: my children, Esther and Jesse, for computer confidence; Jean Rowell for clerical support; John Lowe for his patient attention; Lotte Shankland and Nigel Mellor for their critical friendship and Hugh Shankland for taking photographs which capture the moment of communication that counts.

List of contributors

Jill Atkinson qualified as a teacher at Chester College. She has worked as an early years teacher in a variety of nursery settings in Tyne and Wear and at the Child Development Centre at the Royal Victoria Infirmary at Newcastle upon Tyne. She obtained a BA (Hons) at Northumbria University in 1996. She is currently the teacher at I CAN North Tyneside.

Tina Cook was head of a pre-school service for children with special educational needs in Newcastle upon Tyne in the early 1990s. Prior to this, her experience as a special educator was varied. It included working with young offenders in social service settings and working abroad with children with a range of learning difficulties and emotional and behavioural problems. She has taught in remand and assessment centres, support services and mainstream schools. She currently lectures in early childhood studies at Northumbria University.

Dorothy Edwards is qualified with an NNEB in Nursery Nursing. She has ten years' experience of working in a mainstream nursery and during this time took a post-qualifying diploma. She is now the SSA at I CAN North Tyneside and has recently studied as a Speech and Language Therapy Assistant, gaining a BTEC qualification.

Marion Farmer obtained her first degree in psychology at Birkbeck College after an initial period as a teacher of music and infants. She then trained and practised as an educational psychologist in the North East of England, spending some time working in a school for children with communication disorders. She completed her PhD at Newcastle University. Currently she is a Senior Lecturer in psychology at Northumbria University and continues to practise as a consultant educational psychologist. Her research interests lie in the area of language difficulties and social cognition.

Fleur Griffiths shares her time between working as an educational psychologist in North Tyneside and as a senior lecturer in Early Childhood Studies at the University of Sunderland, School of Education. Her initial degree was in English Literature (London University, 1961–64) and her first teaching post involved her in team teaching of topics, using story, art, dance and drama. She quickly focused on children with special needs.

She developed a specialist interest in language acquisition and disorder, which she brought to her work as an EP. She has practised in the North East since qualifying in 1979 from Queen's University of Belfast and has had particular responsibility for language units and parent involvement in literacy schemes. She is currently part of a multi-professional team, working in a specialist nursery for children with communication difficulties and also runs a weekly support group session for parents.

Marysia Holubecki is currently working as team leader of a Behaviour Support Service, supporting schools with children of all ages who are presenting with challenging behaviour. Previously, she has worked with children with special educational needs. Her particular interest is in communication difficulties, approached from a background in philosophy, especially semantics and theory of meaning. She is presently undertaking MSc studies on communications styles at Sheffield University.

Stephen Laws is a parent whose son Jon came on one of the I CAN projects. He is a houseparent and novelist and a major contributor to parents' groups.

Sheila Liddle is a retired teacher whose experience spans the full school age range. Although she specialised in Music and Science Education, from the outset her chief focus has been on children in need. For her last appointment, she joined the team at the pre-school nursery for children with speech and language difficulties in Sunderland (the I CAN Pilot Project of 1989). She is currently near completion of an MPhil, drawn from this last experience.

Nigel Mellor is an experienced educational psychologist in North Tyneside LEA with a wide range of interests covering in particular low stress approaches to reading, attention-seeking behaviour and 'messy' research methods.

Di Nicholson trained both as a speech and language therapist and as a teacher. She has worked in a language unit in North Tyneside and now works for Northumbria Healthcare Trust, offering support to groups of children and their teachers in mainstream schools.

Emily Partington qualified in 1996 from Newcastle University and worked as a generalist speech and language therapist for South Tyneside Healthcare Trust before joining I CAN North Tyneside pre-school service in 1998.

Judy Waters is a specialist educational psychologist for early years in Newcastle upon Tyne LEA. Her particular interests are communication disorders and play-based and dynamic assessment. She has been a Parent Partnership Officer and continues to encourage parental involvement in assessment and intervention for young children.

Bev Wilson qualified as a speech and language therapist from Newcastle University in 1998 and has worked professionally since then with Northumbria Healthcare Trust. She particularly favours work with parents using the Hanen approach to communication.

Foreword

Benita Rae Smith

When Lucie Anderson-Wood and I were writing *Working with Pragmatics* in the early 1990s, we firmly believed that children's understanding of the world is socially constructed and that, when the ability to interpret is impaired, intervention needs to be fundamentally social. However, we were aware that colleagues were trained and professionally encouraged to focus their efforts upon language and its impairment rather than upon relationships. Pragmatic knowledge, at that time, was seen as an optional extra which might be attended to if there was time available. The weakness of this approach is that children who have not yet acquired an understanding of how conversation works are unlikely to acquire this understanding from purely language-focused interventions.

So for us *Communication Counts* is an encouraging book. It appears at a time when the tide is changing in language remediation studies and provides research evidence for this change, practical guidance for day-to-day work with children and suitable references to pursue for support.

In recent decades professionals working with children who find it difficult to communicate have spent a troubling period of restriction and doubt. We have attempted to clarify our thinking, refine our analyses and, above all, to set aside emotion and folklore when dealing with these children and their problems. Some of these efforts have benefited the children and their families, of course. It is no bad thing to think critically or to submit our thinking to a degree of discipline. Intuitive approaches do need to be subjected to honest scrutiny and fortified with scientifically derived information if problems that do not yield to their application are to be solved.

These developments, however, have had their disadvantages. Communication is an inter-subjective event, but science demands that we attempt objectivity. Unfortunately little children can find it hard to pick up the pragmatic rules of interaction from adults who prioritise a scientifically constructed pedagogic agenda in relating to them and this is what some professionals have sought to do. Attention has also been focused on speech and language, about which we now know a good deal, rather than on the art of making communication work, about which our knowledge is more fragmented.

In this book the participants in the 'dinner dialogues' show us, in detail, how to lay a firm foundation of real communication, even with 'difficult' children, before they are asked or expected to open themselves to language acquisition or to take on the laborious tasks of supplementing a possibly faulty language acquisition system through direct instruction.

We are shown some helpful approaches to the notoriously problematic area of pragmatic assessment. How can teachers, psychologists and therapists capture the essence of a person's communicative abilities and resist pressures to provide only measurable samples of those abilities? How can the views of a subject's closest associate and family members about that person's day-to-day interactions come to have equal status with the results of formal testing for the purposes of placement intervention and even research? This book begins to answer those questions in a way that offers potential benefit to both children and adults.

The troublesome issue of reading is also explored, together with its links to anxiety and to communication needs and desires. It was a joy to find a cheerful and positive approach, born out of long experience, which might relieve the stress that many teachers report in connection with this vital topic. It is not only children who worry about reading and writing. How constructive it would be to review the country's literacy policies in the light of this chapter.

One of the shortcomings of late twentieth-century approaches to speech, language and literacy remediation was that consideration of powerful factors such as emotion and personal involvement could be ignored, or somewhat impersonally dealt with under the distancing guise of 'affect'. In this book, however, the feelings and perspectives of families, professionals and children are shared and respected, which suggests to me that interventions based on the principles emerging from the 'dinner dialogues' stand a good chance of success.

With the publication of this book our work is taken forward and professionals are offered clear guidance and support for remembering that real communication counts.

Introduction

Value should be placed on contexts, communicative processes, and the construction of a wide network of reciprocal exchanges among children and between children and adults.

(Malaguzzi in conversation in Edwards et al. 1998: 68)

To make sense of the chapters that follow, the contexts in which this book has been socially constructed need to be explained. This is in keeping with the central theme that language develops in natural environments with key people and that children with communication difficulties need facilitative play partners in dialogue on matters of joint interest. The theory of social constructionism fits with the experience of the early years practitioners contributing to the exchanges at the heart of the book (see Marion Farmer's review in Chapter 9).

We have taken heart from the complementary experience of Reggio Emilia which upholds a structure in the education of young children 'based on relationship and participation' and which seeks continuously to 'maintain and reinvent a network of communication encounters' (Edwards *et al.* 1998: 66). The system of relationships is not some kind of 'giant security blanket' or some kind of 'flying carpet that takes children to magic places'; it is 'a permanent living presence always on the scene, required all the more when progress becomes difficult' (Malaguzzi in conversation in Edwards *et al.* 1998: 69).

Social contexts

On a weekly basis, four professionals (I am the educational psychologist on this team) work on a particular initiative to enable the settings, i.e. the home, the mainstream nursery and the specialist classroom of pre-school children judged to have specific language difficulties. The national charity I CAN set up and funded the initiative in the beginning in partnership with the local authority, and later taught us to be trainers. Reflective commentaries on this work are expressed in Chapter 5, entitled 'Mind the Gap: Between Theory and Practice'. The case studies and stories which emerge provide illustrative back-up throughout. Permission has been sought and names have been changed if such confidentiality was wanted. Parents also comment on the value of the partnerships with professionals they have experienced on this particular project.

Apart from this current working context, a group of practitioners, with whom I have had the honour to work in a variety of situations since coming to the North East of England in September 1979, has met regularly over the past year to converse about matters of concern. These conversations have fuelled the discussions in the text. We were willing to bring our various perspectives together around the dinner table.

Dinner dialogues

Each time I listen to the conversations taped at the first meeting of colleagues round the dinner table in my house on a dark November Friday evening, at the end of a week's work, I am struck by their energy and commitment to children with communication difficulties. I had the microphones clipped to the tablecloth and people were so engaged in the topic that the conversation remained focused for hours with little sign of inhibition apart from the occasional lowering of the voice or the 'Don't record this!' We were aware of the "messiness" of such a method of collecting data. As well as the technical difficulties arising from the competing noises of rattling cutlery, clinking glasses, thumps on the table for emphasis and even ironic cheers and loud laments, there are the difficulties of disentangling interrupted trains of thought, people speaking at once, or excitedly taking more than their fair share of the conversation.

Even so, each of us had an ocean of memories, thoughts, opinions, observations, anecdotes to bring, and so little time or opportunity to share or debate them in a warm, empathetic and respectful climate. We were joined by frustration over restrictive systems and stilted practices in our educational contexts. We shared a trust in the power of enabling relationships, at the heart of teaching and learning.

To make sense of these confusing but coherent dialogues was the aim of this exercise. Apart from the sense of well-being that springs from sharing experiences – so many of us work in lonely contexts as teachers, support teachers, therapists and psychologists – we were committed to the notion that insights are born in the heat of social situations and meanings are socially constructed. We were confident that the group would spark off ideas and trains of thought, latent in our experience, which we would normally struggle in solitude to articulate from the myriad voices in our minds! We saw thought as internalised conversation. New conversations would create further layers to the structures we had already created. Classical 'dialogues' were set pieces with the expert prompting the stooge to open up a field of debate. Our conversations were more egalitarian and avoided question and answer formats that so often characterise classroom interchanges and research interview schedules.

From our conversations emerge the themes and preoccupations which form the content of this book. We have been given the chance to communicate, on the one hand, certainty about positive outcomes of work with children, and at the same time, to venture doubt and concern about unreflective practice, unresearched dogmas or political slogans. Concerns are expressed about educational rulings that judge outcomes at the expense of processes, and quick fix strategies rather than long-term commitment to relationship building. Comments show awareness of the tension for teachers between the push to raise standards and the rhetoric to be inclusive. How best are children with special needs to be included? How can adults support and partner them in their play and facilitate their communication? How can their needs be assessed and addressed without recourse to deficit models? How can we escape being implicated in a pathologising tendency that labels and medicalises special needs? What is good quality practice and how can such things be measured? There is the fear that because we cannot measure values like trust, respect, warmth and positive regard, we value only what can be measured and counted. If we are in favour of observation in naturalistic and interactive contexts, how do we focus on communicative rather than purely linguistic factors?

The conversations in their complexity defy neat analysis and categorisation, but they reveal the intricacies of communicative intent and the urge to construct joint meanings. Our attempts to make sense of our shared contexts in education find a parallel in the processes we engage in with children.

Issues of authorship

In embarking on a collaborative enterprise, I am aware that no one person can reliably speak for another. However hard I try to represent the perspectives of others, it is difficult to be truly collaborative and egalitarian. The power of the authorial role can subvert meanings. Certain collaborators have chosen to write their own texts and others have been happy with a process of agreement with my version of our conversations. I have chosen quotations to give the participants a voice, but my selection plucks the sayings from their full context and inserts them into a frame that carries my meanings. It is, inevitably, my voice that makes sense of the whole: 'It is in the transaction between objective conditions and personal frames of reference that we make sense. The sense we make is what constitutes experience' (Eisner 1993, cited in Hammersley 1993:53).

As a psychologist coming from positivistic science, I am aware of the dangers of subjectivity and the lack of reliability and validity of soft data and anecdotal evidence. This training has at times led me to adopt a defensive tone about narrative approaches. But, in this book, I take the liberty of asserting with confidence that what I have found *works* in rigorously reflective practice over a working lifetime. I am 'warranting a knowledge claim' (Bennett *et al.* 1997: 25) by presenting reflective considerations on practice.

I wish to avoid sterile arguments that arise from entrenched dichotomous positions, which have bedevilled educational thinking. For example, I am not pitting informal play assessment against standardised psychometric assessment, or real books against phonic approaches to reading. I am in retreat from mono-explanations, and have a mind that generates more questions than simple solutions. My cast of mind favours story-telling to communicate the ambiguities and yet the sense of experience. Issues are therefore addressed in 'a narrative style which attempts to communicate something of the messiness of everyday social situations rather than claiming an absolute veracity of events' (Billington 2000a: 4).

I have deliberately quoted Malaguzzi's metaphors at the beginning, because I am sure that figurative language communicates the more strongly. During 'the heyday of logical positivism, literal language reigned supreme' (Ortony 1993: 1), and contributed to a disparagement of figurative language in scientific discourse. It was seen as emotive and as such to be invalid and unreliable for argument, and more suited to the realms of poetry and fiction. It was as if metaphor was seen as a decorative ornament rather than as having a crucial role, intrinsic to language acquisition. I hold that metaphorical concepts are grounded in our physical and cultural life, and create the shared meanings we live by (Lakoff and Johnson: 1980). Sometimes, we are so used to certain expressions that we fail to appreciate their metaphorical status; we take as a matter of fact what is a matter of meaning. We may need to rethink certain metaphors like the delivery metaphor to characterise the curriculum or the computer-processing model for language functioning. We may wish to discard the funnel metaphor and take up the weaving metaphor (Carr *et al.* 1998) to make better sense of the teacher–learner relationship. To understand conversation, we may need to change 'the metaphors of childhood learning from interiorisation to participation' (Pontecorvo 1998).

Difficulty in absorbing the metaphorical nature of language characterises semantic–pragmatic problems, and the thesis proposed in this book is that understanding at this basic symbolic level occurs in active participation in communicative exchanges. These ideas are furthered in Chapter 2: 'Creating a Sense of Self: A Key Role for Metaphor and Narrative'. Extended metaphors help to illuminate important points in each chapter, which can be read in isolation or in a different order. Some of these allegories emerged in our conversations (e.g. horse whispering to illuminate sensitive approaches to behavioural difficulties).

Introducing colleagues in conversation

A flavour of our mutual concerns can be tasted in the following quotations, which serve to introduce our collaborative network of colleagues:

I want to find an evaluation process that works for everybody. (Tina)

What worries me is divorcing assessment from practice . . . it should be rolled into one because what is it for if not to help the development of the child? (Tina)

If assessment isn't interactive – a piece of interactive work in its own right – then what is it? (Marysia)

My feeling is that if you are in a role as a psychologist or a speech and language therapist, where you are in and out in a short time, you can end up doing very artificial things. (Fleur)

Whilst assessing children, I give a lot of feedback and dialogue with them, because I personally don't feel comfortable having somebody sitting in front of me while I just give them task after task to do. I can't actually personally do that and it is possibly a reflection on my personality as much as anything else. (Di)

One of the things I think children need is . . . a bit of the person that is with them giving a bit of themselves. (Di)

Subjectivity is where it is at, as with so many of these things. (Marysia)

By consistency I mean consistency of approach and attitude and relationship . . . and if kids have got that, they will be very flexible. (Marysia)

I think it is very sad that we are managing to be more sophisticated in terms of a pure literacy or a pure numeracy difficulty, but not about a language difficulty or misbehaviour that is often associated with it. (Marysia)

It's hard for teachers because communication disorders are not something that stand up and hit you in the face, are they? (Marion)

My feeling is that teachers will get much more idea of how a child is coping, if they can get the habit of watching – observing the child – just as a matter of natural practice. Watch the child's face. Watch the eyes, what's happening in that little one's face and you will get more [information]. You don't need words. You don't even need gestures. You just need to look at that body language and you will know straight-away what the child needs. (Sheila)

I don't think there is a way psychometrically that you can measure things like trust, the willingness or ability to make relationships, self-worth and feelings of confidence and self-esteem, and the awareness of the social environment and emotions – those things that are crucial for communication. (Sheila)

CHAPTER 1

Being a Play Partner

Once upon a time I visited the nursery to see Jim. He was reported to have done nothing for months except drag a train in circles, watching the wheels turn. He had resisted strongly all attempts to move him on to other choices on offer, refusing even to engage in eye contact. I approached and lay alongside him on the floor to share his view. Slowly, I lined up some play people to be passengers and stood them on a station alongside the route. As the train came past I called out that people wanted to get on the train. Jim became aware of me, and glanced at the station. The second time around, the train came to a halt and I was allowed to put on a passenger. Gradually Jim came to expect passengers to get on and off at more than one station. He began to call out 'Get on!' and 'Station'. Next, I put a cow on the track, which does happen in one of the Tank Engine books. Jim smiled as he put the cow out of the way. This game was repeated for the rest of playtime, and then uncharacteristically, Jim grabbed a piece of chalk and drew a circular track. I followed him and chased his lines right behind him. He ran on fast wanting me to keep up as in a game of chase. His teacher was amazed to see him laughing and having fun.

(Griffiths 2000: 75–6)

I open with this story which has been the most memorable part of an article I wrote about being a play partner with children with communication difficulties (Griffiths 2000). Such is the power of story! It arose in response to a question in a parents' support group session. A father was seeking advice about what to do about his son, who would not engage with the speech and language tasks set as homework. Instead, the child had withdrawn into a stubborn, sullen silence and could not be moved from an everlasting preoccupation with pulling trains around and around the track. All this father wanted was to have a conversation with him but tried in vain. Rather than give suggestions and solutions, I simply countered with this account of a recent visit to a mainstream nursery. Since more can be gained from parable than precept, I left the story to speak for itself. The father reported some weeks later that he was enjoying making tracks and playing trains with his lad and was on to other pastimes; he highly recommended the 'train way'. This became a metaphor for being a play partner.

Taking turns to build a rocket.

(5)

(6)

I have not found a better explanation of what a play partner does than the following description, which I have kept with me since it was first published (see also Box 1.1):

> The responsive partner listens to what the child has to say, hands conversation back to the child and allows time to reply. A topic of conversation is sustained by relating each utterance to the child's previous turn and to the context. However limited the child's contribution, a good partner may expand, clarify and paraphrase the child's intended meaning. Empathic responses or social oil encourage the child to say more as do personal contributions. Avoided are high control responses such as drilling, open questions or display questions, correcting, enforced repetition or imitation. The rule of thumb is 'only connect', concentrate on sharing understanding with the child. (Webster 1987: 27)

In our work, however limited the child's verbal contribution, we aim to become responsive play partners, concentrating on connecting with the child's interests. Very often we retrace the development to the stage of non-verbal or proto-conversations, taking turns around a shared focus of attention. 'My turn' to scoop some sand on the turning wheel, and now it is 'your turn'. I choose a puzzle piece and now 'you choose' a piece. You pick a red bead so I do the 'same' on my parallel string. I wait and watch you and then you stop to see what I do to match. Keep the doing of the action intact and then give pause to watch and listen. Keep the alternating sequence. Enjoy being a partner. Share the frown of concentration and the joy of achievement. Thus, eye contact happens and the effects of actions are jointly observed and celebrated. Agency is made clear and sociable. Quite often we need to go back to building and knocking down towers, crashing cars as well as fitting, fixing and mark-making together. Language is fused to the heat of these moments.

When on a first home visit, the items I bring are not test items which I administer, where the child performs (or doesn't) and the parent watches (or butts in) and feels proud (or worried) by the result. The whole intention is to create contexts of mutual support which continue once I have left. All 'toys' are used socially. The family group (often including siblings and grandparents) joins in, taking turns around a shared activity. We play lotto, thread beads, complete jigsaws, match and sort but all as equal partners taking turns. The adults simply comment on their choices and needs as they fit with the joint endeavour. There is no need to direct, question, correct or set tests. I pick the 'same as you' and you take notice. Thus, the facilitative relationship of play partnering is modelled and practised from the outset. The adult, rather than feeling s/he is handing over to the expert professional, is realising the value of what often comes naturally to parents: responding to the pragmatic basis of communication rather than pursuing linguistic functions, divorced from contexts that make sense to the child. Parents are empowered to expand, comment, pour social oil, celebrate or clarify, rather than question and drill. They are responsible for keeping the interchange going, making timely repairs. They generally appreciate the story (once again the story works better than advice) I tell about myself as a young child; how I felt when my grammar was corrected instead of my message being received empathetically. Expecting to be praised for eating all my rice pudding 'which I didn't use to like', I was corrected grammatically to 'used not to'. We all remember how we felt being told to 'Say please and thank you'. So often, children with communication difficulties are passive recipients of such instructions, rather than expressive selves.

Facilitative patterns of play are likely to be revisited in the home once the visitor has gone, and it is good if the children can recognise the same arrangements and routines in play at the nursery. Feeling familiar gives the children a sense of security in knowing the ropes and having an active part to play. Here is the pleasure of anticipation and participation with others. There is less chance of home and school speaking different languages and more likelihood of learning transferring from one context to another. Home and school are building up shared meanings around similar activities. If home visits are seen only as opportunities to pass on professional expertise, the transplant can well be rejected. If instead, dialogue and negotiation and solution-focused talk take precedence, a more powerful parental partnership model comes about.

Since parents tend to agree that what they most want is a *conversation* with their children, they are usually relieved to forgo a didactic role. To become play partners, conversing around joint activities takes the pressure from forcing linguistic exchanges and teaching prescribed lessons. It has been found (Anderson-Wood and Smith 1997: 13) that children who have missed the experience of reciprocal interaction with significant others benefit from 'intensive interactive therapy' of six to eight weeks. They present strong arguments for the priority of pragmatics assessment over other areas of speech and language therapy assessment since, developmentally, pragmatics precedes the acquisition of speech and language skills. These authors assert that it is not enough when helping such children to 'equip them with knowledge of fixed meanings and syntactic constructions. They must learn to converse: to share negotiated meanings with others' (ibid.). They point out that the success or failure of speech acts depends on how cooperatively the 'communication-guessing game' is played (ibid.: 8).

What can look like 'just playing' from the outside has a definite purpose and rationale underpinning such practice (Griffiths 2000: 72). It takes strength from the close analysis made of the to-and-fro pattern of early exchanges between infants and significant others (Trevarthen 1979), and puts joint meaning-making at the centre of language learning (Wells 1987). This turn-taking quality with its alternating of acting and observing around a topic resembles the roles of speaker and listener in regular conversation. Just as nursery rhymes allow shared events to be anticipated, so 'games formats' (Smith 1995) give a chance to focus jointly on an action, and have been shown to enable children on the autistic spectrum to become aware of other players. The actors in the game then share the same meanings and memories (Bruner 1983). Further games can centre on common events in children's lives like shopping and cooking. Such events can be recalled with greater accuracy and it is known that children are more able to keep to the correct sequencing in the telling (Nelson 1985). They achieve better expressive competence because they have something important to communicate to someone who cares to listen and who can infer and flesh out intended meanings. Being understood makes the telling worthwhile.

Games have to involve the child and not be artificial constructs designed to teach linguistic concepts (see Mackay and Watson 1989). For example, children love to play hide and seek, to be lost and found, and this can be the motive that induces them to play. A parent well understood this when she was asked by professionals to concentrate on teaching 'big and little' and she chose to hide objects around the house: she and her son found pairs like a toothbrush and a floor brush; a ping-pong ball and a football. The size of the objects related to their real-life functions and big and little were therefore more readily absorbed. False scenarios, dressed up as a game where we all wait our turn to pick out items, make it very difficult to decide on relative concepts out of context. What is 'little' about a plastic calf in the farm set, when a real cow is so big, bigger than a boy? Why separate plastic animals from clothes unless you need to save the toys from a spin in the washing machine! A child, unable to sort clothes from animals, however many times he has been shown the task in the classroom, might have no difficulty separating buttons from smarties, similar in shape and size but functionally worlds apart. To know what is edible and what is not is a necessary judgement in life and a matter of pragmatic importance primarily. Trying to see through the eyes of the child and to converse with him is a very different matter from deciding what he should know and teaching it.

On another occasion, parents were unimpressed by a video of a semantic sorting 'game' which required six children in turn to respond to the teacher holding up an item of clothing or a plastic animal by indicating in which set/ring to place the object. Parents felt that the children looked bored and unmoved even by the clapping which greeted a right response. They felt that the activity had no meaning for the children. In contrast, the excitement of children playing together with a parachute was contagious and after the adults had played the same cooperative game, a grandparent commented about the children's learning:

> I thought at first that they were just having fun, but I see that they were learning about language like 'under' and 'over', 'up' and 'down', 'fast' and 'slow', 'big' and 'little'. They were also doing what the teacher said and listening. Playing was not doing anything you felt like without any discipline.

Parents could spot the difference between a group activity that was designed to teach a linguistic concept and one in which the children learned incidentally by being fully active in a shared dynamic activity, controlled by the rules of the game and under the direction of the teacher. They only had to see the children's faces and hear their spontaneous speech to judge which activity was the more engaging.

Unfortunately in the field of special needs there has been a favouring of a mechanistic step-by-step transmission of the curriculum in an objectives and targets framework to make good diagnosed deficits. If children do not pick up language naturally, there is an assumption that they will need to be taught it in a behaviourist model. They can then be removed even further from the ethos of play partnerships. I remember being admonished for suggesting a child could pretend to drive a car while running on a track of blocks the group had constructed. I was told that he had semantic–pragmatic difficulties, which meant that his chatting about cars was divorced from the action of his legs and that he could not, by definition, *pretend*. My contention would be that joining with him in pretend play was the best chance of bringing language into the here and now and attaching it to the present action. Here is a case of self-fulfilling prophecy: the label was determining intervention. It is like saying that because autistic children are characterised by lack of imagination, we therefore do not expose them to symbolic play because there would be no point. Refusing to take this as a starting point has led to initiatives designed carefully to include autistic children in play situations with others, taking them through the early stages of interactive exchange. This has achieved some notable results (Wolfberg 1999).

Children within the autistic spectrum are often excluded from language units on the grounds that they fail to register communicative intent. Our experience throws up many examples of such children coming to use language functionally because of their involvement in play with adults. First, they have been helped to achieve pragmatic targets before linguistic ones. The difference can be seen by comparing linguistic learning intentions like:

- to understand and use the prepositions 'in', 'on' and 'under';
- to acquire the vocabulary for the categories of vehicles and fruit;
- to increase length of utterance to include three information-carrying words.

with pragmatic ones like:

- to take turns with a partner building blocks;
- to join in action songs;
- to complete a jigsaw with a friend;
- to offer tea to a newcomer in the home corner;
- to be the caller in a game of lotto.

Frequently the activities embodied in the second list are the means for learning the static forms of the first list. This assumes that the interactive pattern is well established and can be used to enable the learning of missing aspects of language. Instead, for children for whom this does not come naturally, it is necessary to practise pragmatics as a first stage. For them, language is called into play when it is a matter of choosing, offering, requesting, refusing, suggesting, and pointing out interesting events to a companion.

I shall finish with another story, which illustrates how children can give us clues about how best to implement their educational plan. The plan then becomes dynamic rather than mechanistic.

> *Once upon a time, I went on a home visit in order to pass on an individual plan to parents and to see if they could be involved at home alongside nursery in reaching certain targets.*
>
> *When I arrived Rudi's interest was engaged in putting magnetic letters in rows on the fridge. To socialise this solitary activity and make it into a shared event, I quietly came alongside and waited, aware of his sidelong glance towards me. Like him, I took time to choose a letter and then announced that it was 'my turn' and inserted my letter next in line. He adjusted my letter to make it fit exactly to his*

scheme, thereby acknowledging my offering but keeping control of the pattern. Then came his turn, verbally advertised by me. Slowly, Rudi came to wait and watch me insert my choice and straightened it up. We started to rehearse the key phrases: 'my turn' and 'I choose' . . . We carried on in this rhythm until the full set (a full alphabet set) was neatly covering the surface of the fridge, with lines going up, coming down from the top to the bottom. He added 'halfway up' on analogy with his favourite song 'Grand Old Duke of York' whose men marched up and down. We both registered that there were no more letters left and I declared the game 'finished'. I went to sit on the sofa and noticed Rudi sitting there, arms crossed in his lap in a relaxed position and a little smile playing on his lips.

In this one play sequence, with its proto-conversational shape, the set targets in his Individual Educational Plan (see IEP: Table 1.1) were encompassed in one go: Rudi finished an activity; he was aware of positional concepts and he took turns with a partner. It had the advantage of arising naturally from the child's interest in lining up. The adult was not feeding into an unhelpful obsession, but was risking breaking in to it, and forging a new social shape to the activity. Rudi was tactfully led into a social extension of his activity, which took on a communicating function. His plan was respected and he kept the initiative, allowing a partner to join in, safe in the already acquired knowledge of what turns mean. Parents, who have already adopted a visual timetable to bring the comfort of routine to the day, were expecting Rudi to throw pieces about, as normally happens at a certain stage. In the past, they have had to intervene to control or to test his knowledge of letters and colours, only to have a tantrum on their hands. To implement targets were fraught matters as far as they were concerned. They knew that Rudi resisted adult-led tasks and did not take kindly to interruptions and change. When he did not answer or appear to understand what was required, there was the natural temptation to say it again more urgently and overload the language level. Keeping calm, giving pauses and time for him to make sense are helping the exchanges to develop with less but more relevant language being attached. Reducing available materials and putting favourites on view but out of reach, have increased the chances of Rudi having to communicate preferences to them and finishing something before pulling out something else. There is more opportunity to negotiate and model proper use of objects in a communicative frame. Rudi is beginning to feel some pleasure in tasks completed jointly.

'It is through conversation that children are exposed to adult ways of thinking and organising and as a result of pursuing meaning together, children's hypotheses about the language system are both raised and challenged'

(Webster, in Cline 1992: 17).

Table 1.1 Individual Education Plan

Learning Intention	Suggested Activities	Comments/Reviews
Rudi will be able to: Follow positional concepts consistently in a variety of situations	• Everyday situations • In play with miniature people and objects • Pictures – see attached sheet	• Begin with whole body real life. If Rudi has success with real objects in play and in everyday situations then see pictures attached for working with him at a secondary stage
Use play items functionally	• In home corner use telephone for talking, cup for drinking, bed for sleeping	• Adult to model the relationship between objects and move on to simple pretend play sequences
Understand and use a range of action verbs (jump, crawl, kick, throw)	• Rudi to use his body to experience action verbs. Activity to be purposeful e.g. throwing a ball at skittles, kick a ball into a goal	• Adult to demonstrate and *join in play* with Rudi and emphasise the key word
To take turns with another child in a play situation	• Pouring sand/water onto a wheel • Building towers with blocks • Putting pieces in a jigsaw	• Adult to facilitate
To see a cognitive task through to completion	• Jigsaws • Bead threading or following bead patterns • Matching games • Shape sorter	• Adult to facilitate understanding of concept of 'finished' in terms of a cognitive task to be done

Box 1.1 Strategies for language interaction

The strategies listed below have been prepared as a handout for schools and are aimed at enabling a better flow of language interaction between children and their conversation partners.

Ten language principles for helping children with special needs

1. **Create a context for conversation**
   Adults and children do not talk about nothing. They discuss things of mutual concern arising from a shared activity. It is always easier to understand a child's utterances and for the child to understand the adult when talk surrounds a known context. For this reason the home–school diary is invaluable in helping teachers relate talk to home events and so that the family can extend and talk over school activities. Children are much more likely to talk about things which are relevant to themselves and their lives. In a community with ethnic minorities this is an especially important principle when stories, books and topics are chosen.

2. **Comment on the child's play and activity**
   Show an interest in what the child is doing and relate talk to the immediate context, helping the child to explore a topic further. Practical, 'hands-on' experiences are more likely to stimulate talk:

   e.g. You're putting the seat in the car so the man can get in?

3. **Talk with, not at the child**
   Children should be genuine language partners, discussing and negotiating meaning with adults, even at a single-word level. Trying to teach new words or pronunciation out of context usually does not work. Conversation is almost a by-product of shared experience, not an exercise in itself.

   e.g. Child = Ot.
        Adult = Hot? Yes that's the kettle.

   In this example the adult sustains conversation around a topic of mutual concern by checking the child's intended meaning and making it explicit, relating each utterance to the child's previous contribution, expanding and supplying useful vocabulary, and generally negotiating with the child, despite the limited language structure under the child's control.

4. **Be patient**
   Listen with genuine interest to what the child has to say, hand conversation back to the child and allow time to reply. A child can usually be sustained into saying more if the adult gives 'phatic' responses or 'social oil'.

e.g. Hm, that looks interesting.
   Ooh, that looks good.

5. **Don't overload conversation**
When the child gives a word or short sentence, respond by restating, extending and expanding slightly on what the child says.

e.g. Child: Mum go shop.
   Adult: Yes, Mum's gone to the shop for some bread.

Turn-taking, the 'to and fro' of conversation, is helped if the adult includes words which the child has used in the previous turn.

6. **Be personal**
Give personal contributions related to the child's experience and what the child knows.

e.g. Yesterday, I had a surprise too, my . . .
   See, I've fastened your lace.

7. **Don't cross-examine**
Take care with questions when children find it difficult to talk. Test questions ('What colour are your socks?') and open questions ('What did you do at the weekend?') often fail to get any response at all. More helpful kinds of questions for reluctant or language-immature children give an alternative to the child.

e.g. Are they blue or red?
   Do you want me to fasten your button or shall we leave it undone?

8. **Avoid correcting**
Avoid correction or interrupting the child or asking the child to repeat words or a correct sentence. Asking a child to repeat a model ('Say I did, not I done') or correcting faulty pronunciation ('Crisp not cwisp') is usually very inhibiting. Restate what the child is trying to say, but go for meaning rather than correct language. Ask yourself how a normal parent would react to the child who says 'I rided my bike'. Would that be to demand correct grammar, or enquire where the child got to on the bike?

9. **Language is a means to learn**
Not only is language a system, it is also a resource in itself. It is a means to learn other things as well as being learned through use. In the early stages talk will relate to everyday objects, names and activities within the immediate environments. Opportunities for language use will arise naturally out of everyday events at home and in school, such as in PE relating

to body parts, action, movement, time and place; or in changing for swimming there will be a natural demand for pronouns and possessives: 'Whose sock, coat, shoe is this?' In putting toys, books and materials away there will be a demand for prepositions: in, on, under, next to, behind. In cooking, a vocabulary for ingredients and action words like 'shake', 'stir', is required. These are just a few examples of how opportunities for language arise spontaneously and naturally out of the child's experiences in school. Tied to real events and activities, language is more functional for the child because it is not being taught in isolation. The teacher who is aware seizes opportunities to extend vocabulary and reflect what the child is doing at the time.

10. **Approach literacy in just the same way**
    Children approach print with the same expectations they hold of spoken language encounters. Reading for meaning and writing for a real purpose engage the child much more than rote drills or exercises. It is almost always mistaken to try to teach language in isolation, as a subject apart.

    Source: Webster (1987: 27–31)

Box 1.2 The role of the adult

Children use a wide repertoire of talk and operate at a high level of ability when:

Adults are aware of what happens in earlier stages of language development and learn from them. For example, mothers who show the greatest sensitivity during the first months of the child's life, produce the most linguistically able children at one year of age. Interactions between mother and child are sustained when the mother lets the child initiate and end interactions and respond to them (Karmiloff-Smith 1994).

Adults are sensitive to the child's current levels of communication ability and are aware of their interests (Wells 1987).

Adults have a desire to help and encourage the child by listening attentively to them and understanding the child's meaning.

Adults extend the child's utterances and reflect what the child has said back to the child.

Adults are aware of the vital role that the home and family play and enter into partnerships with parents (Tizard and Hughes 1984).

Adults and children know each other well (Bruner 1980).

Adults ask open, genuine questions (questions they don't already know the answers to) about experiences that are meaningful (Kersner and Wright 1993).

Adults do not respond too rapidly to the child's contribution, but give the child time to think and add additional information.

Adults speak quietly in the nursery. The average volume of the speech of adults in the nursery is above normal! (Kersner and Wright 1993).

Adults ask fewer questions and, instead, offer their own speculations and reasons.

Adults ask questions that require more than a 'yes' or 'no' answer or that offer a choice between two options.

Adults understand that too many questions lead to tense and depressed levels of performance, less elaboration from the children and less initiative shown (Wood and Wood 1988).

Adults are aware of children's willingness to contribute information when asked to do so and welcome this.

Adults encourage children to use them as a resource (Bruner 1980).

Adults recognise the importance of observing, recording and assessing children's spoken language.

Adults make full use of real, stimulating and meaningful experiences like trips and outings, especially in the local community.

Adults provide a model of high quality spoken language.

Source: Duffy (1998: 140–1)

CHAPTER 2

Creating a Sense of Self: A Key Role for Metaphor and Narrative

Much as Peter Pan's shadow is sewn to his body, 'I' is the needle that stitches the abstraction of language to the particularity of lived experience.

(Holquist 1990: 28)

Young children with communication difficulties present special challenges. Parents are challenged because their instinctive ways of relating to children, their proficient 'motherese', seem not to work. Researchers can be challenged because the children do not co-operate with a verbal process. As specialist professionals (a team of a teacher, nursery nurse, speech and language therapist and psychologist), we constantly need to reflect on our methods in the face of no clear practice to follow, and this is a daily challenge. As human beings, we pride ourselves on our 'ability to be empathetic, our social living and our rich use of language, our flexibility, playfulness, adaptability, and creativity' – all areas of challenge for some children with communication difficulties (Richer and Coates 2001: 15). How can children who are largely silent and frequently spoken for create a sense of self? When they do venture an unintelligible word, it often slips into the ether and no shared meanings are constructed.

Joining children in their play allows them to lead, to be an agent, to be listened to and valued. In such shared moments of turn-taking, a sense of self is constructed. These largely pre-verbal 'proto-conversations' provide the basis for future language development, and without this pragmatic social start, functional communicative interactions struggle to develop. We have all seen examples of children who pick up (often in a parrot-like way) the forms of language and can produce correct grammatical and syntactical sentences but fail to share conversational topics or show awareness of the other's part in the communicative event. Theirs is solo speech not engendered in playful interaction, and not produced for social purposes. They need to engage in games formats to recreate the 'I' and 'you' (or other) characters in the social drama, which makes for personal identity. In our intervention we seek to provide the play contexts that allow such children to assume the power of the 'I'. Using 'I need . . . I want . . . I choose . . .' they begin to engage in meaningful interactions with others and begin to be seen as characters authoring their own stories.

Telling the story of these interactions has become my preferred way of professional reporting. Sometimes these reports can be dismissed as 'just stories'. At the same time, these stories are often welcomed by parents because they capture the child 'to a T'. So, I have come to assert the value of narrative at several levels: to describe children's encounters in context; to communicate messages to parents and to evaluate intervention. I see compatibility between our way of relating to children, to their parents and to collaborators in an evaluation process.

Parent parables

When asked for advice or explanation, I can usually find a story which deals with the question indirectly. There is a shying away from a didactic role and a deliberate use of parable rather than precept, allegory rather than advice. I learned this from a social worker colleague, Eric Harvey, and his fund of stories have been reproduced in a case book (Beaver 1996). My own experiences find useful parallels such as the train story (see p. 7). The use of 'Once upon a time', the age-old narrative opening, lulls the listeners into the relaxation of childhood and into a ready suspension of disbelief. It opens the doors to imagination and allows insight entry. People see the way without following steps in a logical argument. It is no less true for being cast in a fairy-tale guise. This particular story was told in response to a father's direct request for help to break his child's uncommunicative silence and sterile play routines. He later reported back to me that the 'train way' worked and the metaphor became shorthand for a whole way of being in relationship with another as a play partner.

Parents testify to changes in their children after as short a period as a month of daily two-hour sessions of such dialogues (which is in addition to their normal nursery placement). Initially, parents express a common hope to 'have a proper conversation' with their children and this tends to be seen as a purely linguistic exchange. Later comments like 'He is no longer an outsider', 'He's part of the family instead of being in the corner' or 'He is now going up to strangers and saying "My name is Jake"' suggest that the children are emerging with a social identity and a sense of self.

These comments by parents in a round of evaluations at the end of a course, in response to a simple request for any changes observed in their children or themselves, are biographical vignettes not evaluative remarks. A climate of trust and ease has been established over the preceding weeks and such comments are not so much elicited as are pressing to be said, given the opening. A mother said that she felt she had 'lost an arm' when she woke up to the realisation that the parents' groups were over. The strength of the imagery testifies to the importance of the experience and provides evidence of the worthwhile nature of the intervention.

The narrative quality of playful exchanges

Playful exchanges have narrative qualities in as far as they happen within a time-frame, involve actors taking roles and have emotional impact. Children with communication difficulties need help with all these aspects: they find concepts of time difficult, are often passive rather than proactive and aloof rather than emotionally engaged. My understanding is that it is meaningless for linguistic structures (i.e. verb tenses) to be taught before a pragmatic awareness of time is achieved. How do we sense the passing of time except through events recalled and anticipated? First, one needs to be an agent for an event to assume enough significance to stay in the memory and to satisfy the wish for repetition.

With my own daughter, I recall such a significant event in the first months of life. She was waving her arms and kicking her legs when accidentally she knocked the bell suspended above her crib; there was a moment of stillness and then a deliberate striving to repeat the desired action intentionally and to be in control of this circularity of cause and effect. Catching my eye and smiling approval, this became a shared experience with the beginnings of self-consciousness.

Such moments of agency with a synchronous partner are the foundation of selfhood. In the event of being a self with the other, the particularity of lived experience is stitched to the abstraction of language, much as Peter Pan's shadow is sewn to his body (Holquist 1990: 28). The person is the site for continuity of experience but the other has to be there to be a mirror or reflection. Time is more than an endless succession of events; it is a meaningful construction built from particular patterns of anticipation, pause and rehearsal. We have culturally represented time on a clock face and seen circles of time repeated. The 'tick-tock' marks the rhythm, which can be perceived whether felt, heard or seen (Clandinin and Connolly 1991: 261).

The perception of time passing is therefore cross-modal, and in our intervention, we use tactile, auditory and visual objects to signal a timetable of events. The children then know what to expect and have a secure future based on what happened last time we followed the trail. Narratives are built up around these shared events. Children have been shown to tell more coherent stories with more sophisticated time sequences around events commonly shared in their lives, like going to the supermarket (Nelson 1985).

Again, our children are said to have difficulties with pronouns. Before pronouns are used, the nouns of key people need to be absorbed and one's own name especially. Name games and ways of calling another's attention have to be the starting point of our intervention since some of our special children do not appear to respond to their own names, see their own shadows or recognise their reflections in a mirror or photograph. Given this level of awareness, what is needed is a return to the pragmatics of earliest social interactions: to hide and seek, peekaboo, round and round the garden rhymes. Revived is the rhythmical turn-taking pattern of such prototype conversations, with awareness of the other's turn; the watch, listen, do sequence; the anticipation of a tickle after the 'one-step two-step' march up the arm.

There is laughter and suspense; emotion is inherent in any communication. Tense is inextricably bound up with mood – the subjunctive and indicative mood of my Latin primer. In real-life terms, mood is not merely a linguistic feature, it is the emotional quality of the event. Is the happening entirely predictable? Is there a quiver of doubt and anticipation about what might in all likelihood follow? Timing – with elongated pauses – increases the build-up to the hoped for moment of shared fun. A mixture of doubt and certainty is what makes for social mood.

In thinking about timing and emotion in the development of social interaction, I imagined the first monkey in the world seeing himself reflected in a pool of water, and registering surprise or query, the ! or ? of written communication. If the response is one of fear and flight, nothing further can be learned. But if curiosity reigns, and the reflection is prodded, the movements in the mirror can bring new insight: the beginnings of an 'I' as agent can shimmer. If on first meeting with another monkey, the same interrogatory or exclamatory reaction can bring a copying response, further notions of a self, alike but separate, can tremble. This musing of mine is echoed in the ethologist's awareness of the function of 'watching and wondering' in animal behaviour, once there is no need to survive danger by avoidance (Tinbergen and Tinbergen 1972, cited in Richer and Coates 2001). The importance of a calm and curious gaze is seen; too much emotion can lead to avoidance. Children who avoid the anxiety of eye-contact cut themselves off from social learning. As a rule, human babies are particularly predisposed to be social and language development and selfhood are founded on this intersubjectivity (Trevarthen and Aitken 2001) (see Figure 2.1). Thus, we have time before tense, affect before mood, playful turn-taking before conversational turns, pragmatics before linguistics.

Playfulness sets the foundation for communication and language – learning is rooted in emotional, reciprocal action. The 'as if' quality of playful exchanges could be said to establish a metaphorical grammar. The primacy of metaphor may be difficult to take on board if we have been led to think of literal language as coming first and symbolic layers building on top of this literal basis:

> Most people are not too surprised to discover that concepts like love and anger are understood metaphorically. What is more interesting and I think more exciting, is the realisation that many of the most basic concepts in our conceptual systems are also normally comprehended via metaphor – concepts like time, quantity, state, change, action, cause, purpose, means, modality, and even the concept of a category. These are concepts that enter normally into the grammars of languages and if they are indeed metaphorical in nature, then metaphor becomes central to grammar. (Lakoff in Ortony 1993: 212)

In reading the rare and illuminating accounts of adults with autism or Asperger's syndrome, I am struck by their use of figurative language to explain their position. Donna Williams (1996) states how difficult it is to integrate self and other, the doing and the perceiving at the same time. It is either: all self and no other or all other and no self. It is a 'shutdown in the ability to maintain simultaneous processing of self and other' (ibid.: 129). In a television appearance, she illustrates the different ways of knowing, using diverse marbles in a jam jar and toy cows on a table to play out her thinking. A cow burdened with a lump of plasticine stands for the autistic person who makes a less certain, more wobbly way through life, sensing rather than interpreting, and mistakenly being judged as stupid. These props can be moved about to tell her story in a dramatic, present-time way.

Making one thing stand for another is the beginning of symbolic understanding, the kind of understanding supposedly difficult for people with autism to grasp. Those who do acquire language are commonly said to take language literally and miss metaphorical

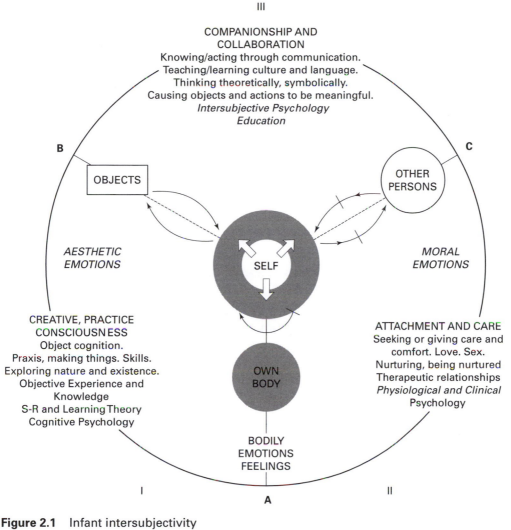

III

COMPANIONSHIP AND
COLLABORATION
Knowing/acting through communication.
Teaching/learning culture and language.
Thinking theoretically, symbolically.
Causing objects and actions to be meaningful.
Intersubjective Psychology
Education

B

OBJECTS

C

OTHER
PERSONS

AESTHETIC
EMOTIONS

SELF

MORAL
EMOTIONS

CREATIVE, PRACTICE
CONSCIOUSNESS
Object cognition.
Praxis, making things. Skills.
Exploring nature and existence.
Objective Experience and
Knowledge
S-R and Learning Theory
Cognitive Psychology

OWN
BODY

ATTACHMENT AND CARE
Seeking or giving care and
comfort. Love. Sex.
Nurturing, being nurtured
Therapeutic relationships
Physiological and Clinical
Psychology

BODILY
EMOTIONS
FEELINGS

I

A

II

Figure 2.1 Infant intersubjectivity
Source: Trevarthen and Aitken (2001: 15)

meanings. Yet here they are using the story-teller's art of allegory, to indicate the feelings rather than the logic of their lives. It looks as if simile can be a bridge from meaningless masses of sensations to a making-sense of feelings recognised and shared. Perhaps the visual similarity helps make the sense, in a narrative rather than paradigmatic mode (Bruner 1986). Perhaps being able to write brings into awareness that which was sensed but was beyond the reach of explanation. In tranquillity, words on the page can be moved about like Donna Williams' marbles or playthings.

Narrative research

Approaches to the study of language and mind can be characterised as mainly 'either dialogically or monologically based' (Wold 1992: 1).

> Dialogically based, social-cognitive approach reflects an insistence on the neces-
> sity to study language use, a conception of the world as multi-dimensional and
> always only partially understood, and man as a social being in search of meaning
> with individual minds embedded in a cultural collectivity. Linguistic meaning is
> conceived as open and dynamic, and constituted in the dialogic process of com-
> munication. It is not to be seen as formal and static representations. (ibid.)

Wold heads a school of linguists who seek to promote Bakhtin's insights about dialogue
being the basis of self-consciousness. Bakhtin, like his countryman Vygotsky, holds that
consciousness of meaning is social in its origin and that thought even in its abstract form
is sublimated conversation. Social situations are the preconditions for reflective consciousness: 'The very capacity to have consciousness is based on otherness' (Holquist
1990: 18). Being is always co-being, a sharing of a moment in time and space. Simply
formulated, a dialogue is composed of an utterance, a reply, and a relation between the
two. It is the relation between the two that is the most important of the three, for
without it, the other two would have no meaning (ibid.: 38). In the exchange comes the
flash of understanding. 'In dialogism, life is expression. Expression means to make
meaning, and meaning comes about only through the medium of signs' (ibid.: 49).

Conversational expression needs to be underpinned by a dialogic model of language
acquisition. Research headed by Trevarthen has demonstrated the primacy of the development of 'self and other' awareness in infancy for subsequent mental growth. He
places person-awareness centrally, not object-awareness which has been the prime
focus 'of individualist, constructivist, and cognitive theory in empirical psychology'
(Trevarthen and Aitken 2001: 3).

Particular research approaches are appropriate for narrative and conversational analysis (see Hatch and Wisniewski 1995). I find in this arena, I can disregard the voice of
the empiricist researcher in my own head urging me to seek representative samples,
safety in numbers, inter-rater reliability, objective stances, and to eschew the dangers of
emotionality and figurative language. Such voices have silenced me in the past and made
me discount the evidence of my experience. Reading feminist researchers and discovering post-modern perspectives within myself have led me to re-value and seek to communicate my experiential findings. I have become aware that there are other legitimate
modes of enquiry, each with particular issues and methodological dilemmas. One such
approach is discussed in *Doing Qualitative Research Differently: Free Association, Narrative and
the Interview Method* (Hollway and Jefferson 2000). These authors see that

> research is only a more formalised and systematic way of knowing about people,
> but in the process it seems we have lost much of subtlety and complexity that we
> often use as a matter of course in everyday knowing. We need to bring some of
> this everyday subtlety into the research process. (ibid.: 3)

To do this, 'the researcher's responsibility is to be a good listener and the interviewee is
a storyteller rather than a respondent' (ibid.: 31).

Doing qualitative research *differently* challenges the assumption that carefully
worded questions can elicit the 'truth' from respondents. Social science research (both

quantitative and qualitative) has refined questioning techniques to avoid 'leading' or imposing meanings. What it has not fully appreciated is the 'defended subject': telling the truth is often too painful and anxiety provoking, and clichés and rationalisations, projections (i.e. Freud's defence mechanisms) distance the versions given from the biographical experience. Using insights from psychoanalytic theory and clinical practice, this line of enquiry values the illogical, emotional connections with sensitive topics (like fear of crime), and posits that only by eliciting personal narratives and allowing these to run freely into associated stories can the complexities, paradoxes and inconsistencies of an individual's meanings be tapped. Later the researcher needs to 'interpret' by following these threads of association, but at the time of the interview s/he needs to listen, and facilitate the personal telling of stories in a relationship of respect, honesty and empathy.

What I have just described mirrors the counselling relationship of Rogers (1961) with his conditions of Empathy, Warmth and Positive Regard. In such a climate it becomes less threatening to the self to admit contradictions and shortcomings. Such revelations are bound to be 'deeper' and 'richer' than responses to set questions on the Likert scale, which yield broad generalisations, and make human diversity a variable which must be averaged out. By telling the story of individuals illuminated by their own 'stories', the authors believe they have captured something of the complexity of psycho-social beings, and by doing this in a systematic and rigorous way they have presented 'more humane and ethical accounts'. Such 'portraits' have the complexity associated with literature and works of art more generally. Hollway and Jefferson trust that their:

> illustrative glimpses of human subjects have respected this complexity: people's struggles with the constraints and possibilities of their social circumstances; their unique biographies; their creative capacities; their ethical impulses; the vulnerability but also the robustness of human psyches in the face of painful, sometimes unbearable assaults on psychological survival. (2000: 155)

The effect of receiving such stories, being a 'vulnerable observer', can be heart-breaking (Behar 1996). No longer is there the immunity of the detached, objective researcher. Questions of confidentiality are heightened. How should intimate disclosures be communicated in writing? Should they be in the public domain at all? However egalitarian the process of data collection strives to be, there is always the power of the authorial voice to contend with. How can transcripts and quotations do justice to the encounter with its timings, conversational turns, emotional colour, back-up gesture, intonation, emphasis, tentativeness, irony and contradictions? The spoken word is more than its pale textual version. What is disclosed is a product of a unique relationship, a particular exchange that cannot faithfully be replicated. Transcription inevitably becomes an interpretative practice, and cannot but be partial with its selection and rejection process. The privileged position of the researcher can mean that the co-respondents are unlikely to quarrel with the written text, unless there are gross misrepresentations.

Being aware of all these issues, I have set about conversing with parents about the intervention with the expressed aim of writing this book about children with speech and language difficulties. Parents want to pass on what they have found useful. In therapeutic contexts, strict confidence is assured. I am used to listening and creating core conditions of counselling and these practices ensure that I will hear a complex story. I am not likely to be fobbed off with a thin, rationally driven version in response to set questions. When I turn public narrator, however, I face the dilemmas of the narrative researcher: new angles on ethics and confidentiality. I now seek the permission of the storytellers to re-tell their stories without being able to guarantee who will read them. When I come to write, I am struck by the inadequacy of the transcript: it lacks the pregnant pause, the emphatic gesture, the vibrancy and tremor of the voice, the search for corroboration. It is a shadow of its former self. The emotional colouring and the quality of the participation are bleached out. To quote parts of the full text is a further dilution of the communication. Selection and omission mould the original into new shapes. Quotations naturally highlight telling passages and rarely include a consideration of the other's role in the conversation. It is hard to render the quality of participation in a dialogue. It requires creativity and sensitivity to re-tell such conversations from their taped versions. Veracity of the account arguably depends more on literary skill than on the application of scholarly research techniques. Not wanting to fragment the flow of the whole experience, the narrator wants to avoid splitting the experience into categorical boxes or reducing complexity to a catalogue of skills or tactics.

So the tape-recording which follows is a deliberate seeking of reflections about our intervention, looking back after a two-year gap. The father and I both know that the encounter is no longer a therapeutic one but serves the interests of written communication in a published work. We are deliberating together on the value of past experience shared at critical points in his child's life. He was concerned to give me what I wanted and I was concerned that he would have the space to articulate his own thoughts and feelings without my imposing a constraining structure. I wanted to be the kind of listener who allows the story to be told. He had had time beforehand to consider what he would like to impart but in the context of an empathetic conversation, dialogues can take unexpected turns because of their dynamic nature. Spur-of-the-moment connections arise. In spite of the artificiality of tape-recording (and my inexperience with it) and the necessary interruptions to cater for children's needs, the interview kept its dialogic shape and dynamic.

What was striking in this context was the use made of narrative. Explanations were couched in telling anecdotes and analogies. The opening remark was an explicit metaphor about depth charges stirring the subconscious into reaction:

> Stephen: *Time's turned elastic for us since things have started moving for Jon. There are times when I can't believe it's two years since he was actually at the project, but when you said you were going to come round and have a talk, it gave me a chance to sort of focus some things from my own point of view – so I've been thinking for the past couple of weeks. It was an enormous step forward for Jon, attending the two placements. During the first one, not a lot seemed to be happening; but that was okay because we weren't really expecting anything to happen – certainly not miracles – but the second one was the one that really did the business for him.*

From a personal point of view, I still can't get away from this metaphor I came up with at the time about depth charges. Do you remember talking about that?

Fleur: Oh yes, yes.

Stephen: It was just like that. It was almost as if, during that first placement, the staff were dropping depth charges in Jon's psyche – his subconscious – and you know, they were hitting the water; they were going down deep, but nothing was happening. Just like those old shots you see on World War 2 documentaries. But then, with the second placement, it was as if the bombs were going off under the water. And the bubbles were coming up, you know, to the surface. Really strong. And I remember how amazed we were when he started to react, when we didn't expect him to react.

Later, a biographical incident was told to illustrate the play way to communication: he put 'something to the test', which he had learned in the parents' support group.

It was at a leisure centre where a child's birthday party was taking place and all his classmates, Jon included, had been invited – and there was another child there who had autistic traits. He was very much more withdrawn than Jon was. I'd gone off by myself to read a paperback book while Jon was playing with the other kids, and the other mothers were sitting together having a chat. But this other child I'm talking about wouldn't play and join in – he'd go and sit facing a wall and be completely withdrawn. His mother kept getting embarrassed at this, dragging him to the other kids. But he'd just come back and face the wall. I was sitting not far from him and I noticed he was doing the stuff that I've learned about – you know – fascinated by the woodgrain on this bench that he was sitting on, and I remembered the business about the play way. So I took a coin out of my pocket and I started spinning it in my hand deliberately until I'd caught his eye. And as soon as I caught his eye, I didn't do the eye-contact thing with him, I deliberately took no notice of him. I started spinning the coin on the table – just spinning it – and I saw him watching. He came over and sat beside me, and still deliberately not doing the eye-contact thing but just, you know, drawing him in, I said: 'Heads or tails?' He said nothing. Right, that's fair enough – he might not get the concept. So I spun it again and I said: 'Say "stop!"' And he said: 'Stop!' – and I slammed the coin down and he laughed. So we spent about fifteen minutes doing that and, bit by bit, we got an eye-contact thing going. That was the project idea, about playing and bringing him in, you know, with the bridges and stuff and – it wasn't a miracle or anything – but he was opening up.

At the end of our talk, I asked whether the same Jon was there from the beginning or had he changed?

Stephen: The whole process he's been through and where he's at now has brought the Jon that we know out into the new world. So he's not changed. It's just brought him out into the world.

We knew him in a kind of body-language way, and learned what he was like then. But as he's now learned to communicate, you can see the Jon that we know and love instinctively just emerging and connecting and communicating – bit by bit – with the outside world. And it's great to see that happen! So he hasn't changed, he's always been there. But now he's emerging.

Jon's parents honour and accept his personality and its difference as can be seen by the concluding story:

Stephen: (I shouldn't say this) We sometimes laugh about Jon being the boy from Mars. It's like the ET thing, you know, where ET lands from outer space, and he gets left behind; the space ship takes off. Well, Jon's like that – the boy from Mars – and of course as Martians go, he's incredibly clever. But what's happened is – well, it's the earth people that he's living with who are stupid. We're the stupid ones and so it's beholden on his Mum and Dad and everybody around him to learn Martian. So what we have to do is learn his ways – and it's amazing, I think, to see in his eyes how well we've come on!

This final story was not pre-planned but sprung up in the context of the dialogue and it was introduced tentatively with the 'perhaps, I shouldn't say this'. It was prompted by my retelling of my first visit to see Jon and his father at home, two years previously. I recalled that Jon was absorbed in a television programme of children singing and doing the actions; he was joining in with them exactly, so precise was his memory. Rather than interrupt or intrude, I decided to place myself as if I were a character on the screen, and to face Jon, doing the same songs and actions. I ventured out of the screen gently to touch his fore-finger, which he had extended to do his beloved counting. I knew how numbers were as people to him. A fleeting smile registered this connection as a communication he favoured. It was like the ET touch with a significant charge. Stephen said he remembered the visit well because it pleased him that Jon had 'connected' with me. Afterwards, he struggled to think how this had come about when it had never done so before with strangers. Now, with hindsight, he reckoned it was 'something to do with body language' and 'the way of approaching' tactfully and playfully as described in the coin-spinning encounter. Luckily, Jon was calm enough to let us see in his eyes that we were on his wave-length.

Perhaps Stephen's figurative modes of explanation reflect my own story responses to parents' questions. Perhaps the listener brings out the storyteller. Perhaps narratives fit more closely to the 'lived experience'. Or perhaps such narratives simply highlight the primacy of storytelling as a way of making sense of complex experience (Novak 1975: 175).

CHAPTER 3

Agitation over Assessment: New Angles on Old Agendas

I am thinking of a little boy I went to see at home, following another professional who had completed a full assessment report on his abilities, showing how far below his age level he was functioning. Mother had set out jigsaws to demonstrate what her son could do and she tried to get him to perform and show off his clever side to me. There was resistance and tantrums. I could see mother getting more and more agitated and I just said, 'Leave him; he's all right.' The next thing you knew, he was sidling up to help me do his puzzle and beginning to co-operate and do things his mother knew he could do. She said, 'You know why he is doing better? It's because you like him.'

(Fleur in conversation)

I don't think there is a way psychometrically that you can measure things like trust, the willingness or ability to make relationships, self-worth and feelings of confidence and self-esteem, and the awareness of the social environment and emotions – those things that are crucial for communication.

(Sheila in conversation)

I thought, 'How can I assess him?' He didn't want to be there because it was Christmas and there was a great, big Christmas tree standing next to him. So, I did the assessment on the Christmas tree. We looked at all the things that were hanging on it and I could test his comprehension: 'Show me . . . and point to'.

I could do a speech assessment within reason from the conversation. I could move him on to related things and he didn't mind. So, at the end, I hadn't used one thing out of my box. I just used stuff that was in the classroom and I knew pretty much what was the matter because it was fairly straightforward. That's just using contexts.

(Di in conversation)

These conversational comments serve to introduce the themes of this chapter on the assessment relationship. There are first of all concerns about 'assessment failures' (Waters 1999) and the anxieties which arise for parents from normative judgements

Joint attention while practising lip-rounding and blowing.

Before he came here, he would not have tolerated standing close to someone. There seemed to be a barrier between him and others. A whole new world has opened up to him. He spoke no more than a few words, but now he is coming out with words spontaneously. He is so confident and happy. This is the same in his nursery: he's mixing in more and taking part at story time. He is keen now to laugh and have a joke! He can now make things happen and be the actor in his story. He was even (when we were not looking) telling the story to his teddy, tucked up with him, with all the dramatic sound effects and actions. (Parent) about their children. Further concerns revolve around the inadequacies of formal stan-dardised assessments both to uncover communication difficulties and to encourage ideas for intervention. I attempt to show the dangers of working in sealed off compart-ments, unmindful of the gathering emotional effect of assessments carried out for different purposes on the same subjects. To combat some of these dangers, there need to be more flexible and creative ways of assessing and helping.

More interactive, play-based assessments relieve both professionals and parents from such frustrations, and absolve children from being called 'untestable, uncoopera-tive, unintelligent or hard to reach'. We can move from deficit to empowerment models of practice. We can use the power of seeing from multiple perspectives and of engag-ing parents and children as true subjects and not as passive objects to be investigated. Participants with shared responsibility can replace respondents.

We can adopt Joan Tough's approach to cultivating conversations with children and favour her terminology when she uses 'appraisal' instead of 'assessment' and 'fostering' in place of 'intervention' so that the two are inextricably entwined (Tough 1977). As she says: 'The approach we take is not that of teaching language but one of fostering skill in communicating through the use of language' (ibid.: 4). If discovering what children know and how they can learn is our educational aim, then we must keep up a dialogue with them. This outlook is founded on the belief that there must be respect for the child and an attempt to understand his view. If the child is given experiences with adults in contexts that have immediate or potential interest, then the child can come to return that respect. A relationship is then established that is based on the concern of each par-ticipant in the dialogue to be understood and to understand the other. This is not a soothing mantra; it is a demanding commitment to a taxing set of conversational strat-egies for adults (see the framework for fostering children's use of language, Box 3.1).

We can catch the informal moment in chance contexts as they arise as with the Christmas tree assessment above, or we can adopt charted interactive methods, which go beyond rigorous observation to joint working with a clear procedure. Such approaches have been derived from dynamic assessment, which focuses on the process of learning between a child and an adult mediator (Lidz 1991). A local application in the assessment of pre-school children using play comes in the shape of a Bunny Bag of toys (Waters and Stringer 1998). The New Zealand curriculum pattern (Carr *et al.* 1998) creatively allows a purposeful use of stories for assessment and evaluation; the nursery teacher can assess, record and plan directly in the course of daily encounters with children. Holistic, interactive approaches have been developed with professional collaboration in what has been called transdisciplinary play-based assessment (Linder 1993). It has produced detailed checklists which can be used by the team. Linder pro-vides an alternative system to replace the fragmented, often duplicated efforts which exist if each professional pursues a lonely furrow.

A pathologising culture

The following is a worst case scenario, but not unusual or fabricated. Well-meaning pro-fessionals, carrying out assessments of special needs in the home, can sow the first

Box 3.1 A framework for fostering children's use of language

1. Self-maintaining strategies
1.1 Referring to physical and psychological needs and wants.
1.2 Protecting the self and self-interests.
1.3 Justifying behaviour or claims.
1.4 Criticising others.
1.5 Threatening others.

2. Directing strategies
2.1 Monitoring own actions.
2.2 Directing the actions of the self.
2.3 Directing the actions of others.
2.4 Collaborating in action with others.

3. Reporting on present and past experiences strategies
3.1 Labelling the components of the scene.
3.2 Referring to detail (e.g. size, colour and other attributes).
3.3 Referring to incidents.
3.4 Referring to the sequence of events.
3.5 Making comparisons.
3.6 Recognising related aspects.
3.7 Making an analysis using several of the features above.
3.8 Extracting or recognising the central meaning.
3.9 Reflecting on the meaning of experiences, including own feelings.

4. Towards logical reasoning strategies
4.1 Explaining a process.
4.2 Recognising casual and dependent relationships.
4.3 Recognising problems and their solutions.
4.4 Justifying judgements and actions.
4.5 Reflecting on events and drawing conclusions.
4.6 Recognising principles.

5. Predicting* strategies
5.1 Anticipating and forecasting events.
5.2 Anticipating the detail of events.
5.3 Anticipating a sequence of events.
5.4 Anticipating problems and possible solutions.
5.5 Anticipating and recognising alternative courses of action.
5.6 Predicting the consequence of actions and events.

Projecting* strategies

5.7   Projecting into the experiences of others.

5.8   Projecting into the feelings of others.

5.9   Projecting into the reactions of others.

5.10 Projecting into situations never experienced.

Imagining* strategies

5.11 Developing an imaginary situation based on real life.

5.12 Developing an imaginary situation based on fantasy.

5.13 Developing an original story.

* Strategies that serve *directing*, *reporting* and *reasoning* serve these uses also.

seeds of worry. That seed is fed and watered by a succession of professionals, each trying to probe what is wrong and perhaps to justify a disability label. Evidence gained strengthens the case for a particular diagnosis and then for selection for particular interventions, designed to make good revealed deficits. Too often, the parent watches anxiously on the sidelines, not permitted to help and not daring to dispute professional expertise. The tests are seen (often mistakenly) as helpful in deriving plans for improvement. More often, they provide justification for segregation for special help. Once selected for the special help, the same child can be tested again by researchers, for the purposes of establishing base-line data, against which the success of the intervention can be judged. The need for post-intervention measures means more testing. Watching parents are then used as informants to judge the benefits of the therapy. The team of practitioners continues to assess in order to acquire leads for intervention. At the same time the team knows its own efforts are being evaluated and perhaps being found wanting. Comparisons are being made with other teams. Like the parent, the professional is now not fully in the know about the purposes of the assessments or the kind of proofs, which are being constructed by the research team. After all this, if the child is shown not to have made sufficient progress, another round of formal and statutory assessments with another band of assessors begins. Before the child is five years old, the seed has grown into a tree of pathology with long roots.

At the outset, I deliberately put this 'battery' (an apt metaphor) of assessment in one frame for one individual to show how easily all of us involved in caring for children with communication difficulties can be drawn into a pathologising culture (Billington 2000: 1–2). I am strongly aware of the dangers of becoming part of the blaming culture, 'For a culture in which children are pathologised is a culture which has at its disposal the capacity to pathologise the adults too, parents, teachers or psychologists, for example' (ibid.: 2–3). Each of us may not be aware of the cumulative effect of our efforts to do our assessments, whether as practitioners or researchers. We are working in our own small corners, going about our own business. In the real world of the child at home, the assessment compartments are not as hermetically sealed; messages leak out and across the borders. An assessment designed to yield evaluative data about a project affects the individual, those around him in the room at the time, and those who will teach him or offer therapy in another room at another time. The parents will want to know how well (compared to others) their child has performed. The practitioners will also want to know their comparative standing. Meanings and interpretations are arguable, and judgements are rife. There is plenty of space for justification and defensive casting of blame.

I have spent (perhaps wasted) so much of my professional life explaining the meaning of numbers (expressed as scores, centiles, norms) when attempting in all good faith to assess and intervene for children with speech and language difficulties. I have done so much mopping up of parental distress caused by diagnostic accounts containing these measures, which leave behind worry rather than a way forward. Morale can plummet at perceived deficits, and excuses and justifications can abound in the face of documented faults and failings. The scientific findings, however valid and reliable, are resisted. Resistance can then be further judged as a failure to 'come to terms with' unpalatable truth. Numbers can be truly numbing!

Instead, bleaching the blame out of situations so that there is energy to agree on how to move forward becomes the major part of my job. (See Billington 2000b: 66–7 for safeguarding principles.)

Deficit models

In our work, it is all too easy to focus on difficulties and get drawn into a deficit model, seeking to make good errors and lacks within the child. Mostly, the deficits have been diagnosed by standardised assessments with their norms. This normalisation approach, so common in special educational needs research, is questioned by Gray and Denicolo (1998), who give a detailed account of the varying research paradigms and the inferences that can and cannot be drawn from particular theoretical research perspectives. They show how so much research in this area falls into the empirical–analytical paradigm, which regards human affairs as containing measurable law like qualities to be identified and manipulated. They argue that this might be 'a flawed assumption and that all researchers need to be aware of the potentially political nature of their position' (Gray and Denicolo 1998: 140). They propose that research should have some 'practical implications' for special needs groups who should themselves become the 'subjects rather than the passive objects of research' (ibid.: 144). Researching individuals in categories of handicap perpetuates a labelling of individuals as the source of the problem rather than seeking to understand the societal attitudes that create such labels. If strategies which engage actively with the 'target audience' are adopted, then 'researchers . . . can begin the often difficult process of positioning themselves on the side of those they seek to help' (ibid.). Such questions have long been debated and yet are as telling still: 'Research is not a value-neutral activity. It is a social experience in which the subjects of research can suffer and perceive particular forms of study as oppressive' (Barton, 1988: 91). Instead, the goals of research should be agreed and understood by the active participants. Researchers need to adopt a 'reflective stance, one that recognises that researchers too have vested interests in the processes and products of their research' (Gray and Denicolo 1998). Ethnography adopts this reflexivity and I favour the following explanation:

> Reflexivity is a social scientific variety of self-consciousness. It means that the researcher recognises and glories in the endless cycle of interactions and perceptions, which characterise relationships with other human beings. Research is a series of interactions, and good research is tuned to the inter-relationship of the investigator with the respondents. (Delamont 1992: 8)

Such a definition emphasises research as a reflective process, 'glorying' in complex interactions and perceptions. The researcher is tuned into the effect s/he is having. Such a description would also cover the self-consciousness and inner dialogue that I would practise, as I try to make sense of the various perspectives I absorb from talking to parents, teachers, children in contexts familiar to them. There seems to be an accord between my reflective practitioner approach and the reflexivity described here.

Varying views on language acquisition

In the field of communication, varying views on language acquisition influence practice and indicate particular research paradigms. Approaches to the study of language and mind can be characterised as mainly 'either dialogically or monologically based'. Linguistic meaning can be conceived of as 'open and dynamic' or 'as formal and static representations' (Wold 1992: 1).

Wold is concerned about the tension between language as a conventionalised system and as specific acts of real communication. Mainstream models have tended to fix on the static descriptions of language, on presupposed literal meanings. She sees the need in linguistics to study real examples of communication actually taking place rather than examples elegantly constructed to illustrate theoretical points. This requires research to spring from real situations. The time, place, and exact context, including what is of importance to the participants, must inform the study. The physical and social contexts in which conversations happen are vital. This brings in a new set of terms like: dialogue, intersubjectivity, perspective-taking, temporarily shared social realities, intentionality and attunement. It demands the creation of a 'dialogic alternative' (Wold 1992) to guide research and inform practice.

Implications of the dialogic alternative in our educational context

This approach has implications for those of us appraising and fostering children by having dialogues with them. Our attempts to draw children into meaningful encounters, to join with their concerns in action, cannot adequately be judged by assessments of individual children based on a formal, static, linguistic model. Even the information-processing model that leads to concepts like input and output modes, receptive and expressive channels, can be restrictive. Tests which claim to tap receptive and expressive areas, and which then prescribe ways to make good deficits in these separate areas are of questionable use. A conversational exchange is dynamic and defies simple illustration with boxes and arrows, inputting and outgoing; it requires almost simultaneous looking, listening, remembering, planning, executing and voicing across quick temporal turns. Normally, children absorb more than they can express and children with language difficulties need skilled partners to maintain dialogue. They need support to keep the turn-taking pattern of communication flowing. The role of the mediating adult – scaffolding the learning; oiling the flow of conversation; putting in timely repairs and reruns; articulating unspoken meanings and gestures – is central.

While recognising that our children with specific language impairments in our special nursery have failed to acquire language naturally, we do not feel they require *artificial*, static language programmes to make up their deficits (Webster 1987). Instead, the aim is to encourage conversational patterns with children struggling to express themselves, regardless of the aetiology of their 'disorders'. Since classification in a medical model is extremely problematic (Dockrell *et al.* 1997; Dockrell and McShane 1993; Rispens and Van Yperen 1997), we wanted to resist grouping children according to 'diagnosis' – separating phonological disorders from semantic ones. We felt that we could benefit from mixed groups since children often had complementary skills. Better chances of conversational exchange of a meaningful kind were forthcoming in such groups with mediating adults.

A contrary view urged us to group children with similar language difficulties together so that an appropriate intervention package could be delivered to them. The idea that with more acute study a more exact diagnosis will be found which in turn will bring more potent remedies fuels much research. In the early days of our project, it was decided to evaluate the benefits of our intervention by conducting a search of this kind, seeking 'to match types and severity of language difficulty with the most effective intervention packages'. In this instance we were prevented from choosing 'sub-types' and applying a particular *medicine* of intervention, because finding such homogeneous groups on tap, ready and willing, was impossible. Whether this was desirable was an even greater issue.

I recorded my concerns in my professional diary thus:

> My concerns arising from this first meeting were as follows:
> (a) how to group children according to type of language handicap as was being proposed
> (b) how to match interventions to 'diagnosed' difficulties
> (c) how to accommodate the requirements of a research focus which had been agreed.
>
> The research student placed with the project speech therapist was already well known and accepted in the group by the time of my first visit. She was expected to carry out an experimental paradigm: baseline assessment – intervention – re-assessment. Data was to be collected which could measure change, as a result of the intervention. The notion of grouping children with phonological difficulties separately from those with, say, semantic/pragmatic problems, served the needs of the research design. As teachers and educators,

we were anxious about attempting group work with groups selected in this way. We are used to differing strengths and weaknesses bolstering and complementing each other. The child with good comprehension can help the child with semantic problems, who in turn provides clear speech models for the one struggling to articulate.

Over and above the wisdom of 'like' groups, is the further problem of finding such discrete categories. With language units, I have not found it easy to make such easy labels – especially with such young children. I am suspicious of research projects which easily assigned children to defined categories, and matched them with controls.

The research, nevertheless, went ahead. The graphs and tables which emerged showed overall gains as measured by the tests of receptive and expressive language, and seemed to point to the success of the intervention. This was heralded as good news. I was concerned, however, because the measures were of language elicited in formal test situations, one-to-one with the examiner, sometimes at home, sometimes in our nursery or neighbourhood nursery. Could such measures reflect the aims of our intervention? Could such data identify what factors contributed to the effect? What aspects of the intervention are responsible for any changes? Is it the specialist input? Increased one-to-one attention? The involvement of the parents? The supportive group? Adult mediation in play? Having fun and being relaxed? A secure structure? Careful assessment and teaching to targets? The particular qualities of the staff?

Incidentally, the researcher noted (from informal conversations with parents and nursery staff) that the children were showing greater confidence to initiate interactions, and were attending better to the speech of others. If there had been a way of measuring the frequency and function of such exchanges, the data would arguably have been more in keeping with the kind of evidence needed to evaluate our way of working. (See Counting Communication, Chapter 4, for an alternative approach.)

A case example: Jim's story

A particular example illustrates what can be lost if a child's competence and improvement are gauged simply by test score gains. A boy, Jim, who registers little change on the linguistic measures, is the child whom we would have heralded as having changed dramatically. The numerical results do not reflect the change in this child's communicative range, observed by parent, staff and mainstream nursery teacher.

Jim's changed way of relating to others was so striking that his case was chosen to relay to other colleagues nationally; it also provided the basis for a story I wove to illustrate for parents how to become a play partner and join with children's interests (see the train story, p. 7). The extent of Jim's difficulties can be gathered from my case notes, gleaned from teacher and parent on school and home visits; they give a bleak and largely negative view:

minimal expressive language; little communication; avoidance of eye contact; not making wants known; playing repetitively with train on his own; resistant to interference or suggestion; unable to sit up and focus on tasks; extremely restless and inconsequential. Little symbolic play.

Over the year in nursery, he had eventually become amenable to routines and compliant with rules. Beginning to trust nursery teacher, calling her name even at home. Apparently impervious to pain – no tears or comfort-seeking when hurt.

At home: very restless, uncuddly from birth, sleeping little. Seemingly not wanting mother's company or help. Up early to play alone – everything out and lined up rather than played with. Impossible to get him to sit still enough to eat a meal at table. Resistant to change and distressed when thwarted. More obedient for male family members . . .

Obsession with Thomas Tank Engine – meant everything revolved around this: clothing, plates, cups etc; ingrained habits of 'play'.

This would seem to be an entrenched situation and one that was not likely to be altered in a month of intervention. Labels of 'hyperactive' (ADHD) and even 'autism' hovered in the wings.

Yet changes in communicative intent were soon noticeable to mother and nursery teacher and were best captured on video. He was seen approaching others with smiles; drawing them to share in his activities; taking turns at the sand tray or water play; looking at and watching others; calling others by name to attract their attention; noticing when one of the eight people in the group was missing; and taking drawings home to show mother. His mother, fearful at first, became a regular member of the parents' group, and made weekly comments about Jim's increasing trust and willingness to join in activities with her. In the last session, I recorded parental views and she commented:

He has improved a lot – listening and talking. He is aware of people now – he has learned all their names. He is not shut off – he wants to join in, he wants to be there. He is now asking, 'What's this?', and nudging me to answer. He used to be hyperactive but he is much calmer. He joins in with me now – he used to do his own thing and ignore me. For me to be in the group has made me feel I'm not on my own.

Her knowledge of the change is 'proved on the pulses' (Keats) rather than signalled by improved test scores.

How can two pictures of the same child be so different? The reason was said to lie in Jim's failure to sit up and do the formal tests. This failure was attributed to lack of cooperation. It was noted that 'behavioural problems hindered assessment', but the answer to such a problem was to seek further research to identify the behavioural difficulties which attend language disability. Never was the suitability of the test questioned, only the variables within the child. Very easily, the child was judged to have 'behaviour problems' that needed to be tackled by specific interventions.

Taking context into account

We know that being unable to express yourself and being misunderstood and thwarted in your desires will produce frustration, and can result in a range of observable behaviours as diverse as temper tantrums, kicking, screaming, biting, rocking, and hiding away, refusal to look or speak. We have had children who have been reported by nursery staff as chewing the furniture, attacking other children, or covering themselves with pillows, and such behaviours make integration very difficult. A different setting like ours which sets out to establish playful interchange (pre-verbal and conversational) has seen such behaviours fade away. So any assessments which fail to take into account context and conditions are bound to be inadequate.

For more than twenty years, the research inspired by Margaret Donaldson (1978) has exposed the dangers of attributing failure and incomprehension to children when the nature of the test and the social dynamics of the testing situation can determine the results. Yet, because of pressure to produce profiles of skills and language competencies as part of assessment, you can come across the ludicrous situation of a child with semantic/pragmatic difficulties being asked to put buttons *on* toy cars or forks *under* the plate. To find out whether he knows 'on' and 'under', we put him through a meaningless activity dominated by the adult with pencil and form, objectively recording responses. The child in question seems content enough to stay alongside and listen to instructions and even gets the right answer at times, yet remains impervious to the praise. His scores on their own are meaningless. The further issue is whether valuable time is being wasted by indulging in such decontextualised, disembedded situations which do not model real pragmatics.

A similar case is made by Wittman (1998) as she describes in detail the formal and observational assessments carried out on Joanna and concludes that the controlled assessment failed to detect the complexity of her language impairment. She could respond passively to formal requests but was less able to cope socially in the living environment. In this case, the tests were not sensitive enough to illuminate her difficulties and gave too positive a picture.

Experts in the field continue to seek 'instruments' which can detect and 'differentiate subgroups of children with SLI' so that 'differential treatment' can be given. There continues to be an honest pursuit of sufficient and sensitive tests, since checklists and specialist opinions are deemed 'not reliable enough or suitably practical for use in routine assessment'. If there are time constraints, it is the 'assessment of spontaneous language' that is omitted. It is claimed that such data 'would have been a desirable addition' but 'time constraints did not allow' (Conti-Ramsden *et al.* 1997: 768–75).

My contention would be that collection of conversational exchanges, far from being extra optional data, is crucial. Noting difficulties in engaging in relationship and dialogue can lead *directly* to mediation strategies. There have been attempts to do just this (Kerbel and Grunwell 1998; Vedeler 1996; Wilcox and Mogford-Bevan 1995). A closer tie between research and practice is thus forged, instead of the unsatisfactory conclusion that 'further research needs to be carried out before treatment plans can be developed and linked to particular subgroups' (Conti-Ramsden *et al.* 1997: 774–5).

Lack of consonance between clinical and psychometric data, I believe, cannot be solved by a search for ever-sharper instruments. It is more likely to happen if we look in another direction to validate more interactional, dialogic alternatives. We need to develop ways of judging how participants view the interactive process.

Involving parents in appraisal and fostering

Often parents are enthusiastic about interventions which do not gain the same approval from more empirical evidence. This lack of consonance between research evidence of effectiveness and the views of users raises serious questions, outlined by Newman (1999) for Barnados in his discussion of evidence-based practice. Although he notes that there is a poor correlation between the strength of user approval and the impact of the intervention as measured by third parties, he claims, 'There is little doubt that models of empirical practice are widely perceived as undervaluing the perspectives and contribution of users' (1999, Highlight no. 170, National Children's Bureau). Because parents and children are less powerful than professionals and academics, it is hard to ensure that their voices are heard. So much dialogue blows away on the wind of the moment. The power is in the pen that can pin down these fleeting insights and record them. That is why I try to make written versions of what parents so eloquently tell me in order to give more weight to their words (Griffiths 2000: 77–8).

I do not lead but allow the parents in closing rounds to tell about changes they have noticed in their children and themselves. Given such an opening to express themselves, parents share new happenings and insights. Their observations of significant improvements in their children's cooperation, confidence and communicative competence come unprompted and unsolicited.

This personal evidence has the ring of truth and validation about it. Yet because of my worry that such data would not be deemed reliable and valid enough, I felt I should evaluate further. I therefore designed a questionnaire to discover if my aim of empowering parents to take on the main work with their children as play partners was being realised in practice.

Parent empowerment

My search was not to elicit parental reports on the benefits/drawbacks of the intervention for their child. It was not bringing them in as expert witnesses of changes created by expert practitioners. If parents are partners, any questions that assume they are passive onlookers, judging success from the outside, rather than attributing success to joint endeavour, will undermine their contribution. There is a danger of turning parental gaze on to how well professionals have fared, rather than on celebrating achievements by the parent and child. In so short an intervention, parents need to be the chief agents for ongoing change and the parents' groups are designed to promote such agency. I can imagine a situation where a parent has contributed so much to improvement, that she will happily and justifiably deny that the experts have done much! This would be a testimony to empowerment rather than a failure of those experts.

My attempt to capture empowerment sought assent and disagreement with such statements as:

> *I got the chance to chat with other parents*
> *I liked meeting other parents with similar concerns*

I felt other parents were supportive
I felt glad that I was not alone
I felt more confident about what to do
I learned from the experience of others
I was able to share my ideas
I learned some strategies to use
I thought up some new approaches myself
I found out what staff were doing
I came to understand my child better
I found out that I was on the right track myself

In spite of the overwhelmingly positive replies, I was unsure about the interpretation of the resulting bar charts. I felt more uncertain with this anonymous numerical validation than with the spontaneous face-to-face testimonies emotionally spoken in the group. When views are canvassed far from my watchful readings of people's emotional and body language, I cannot begin to guess what is meant by their responses. I could not see any waverings or hesitations.

One thing was certain, however, parents valued the intervention in terms of changes in *attitude* rather than in terms of linguistic gains. They valued improvements in communication and family relationships. There is not space here to do justice to the full range of answers, but one instance illustrates the general tenor of responses to open questions.

I now have a new, little, happy, communicative son who loves other children's company and enjoys being in a group. He is a delight to be with, and is so loving and affectionate as opposed to being silent and frustrated.

And in answer to the question: What (if anything) did you get out of coming?

Reassurance that there could be progress.
Knowing that we were not alone.
Accepting our child's problems as not being totally abnormal.
Having a relaxed attitude towards him instead of being uptight and allowing it to dominate every hour of every day.

These comments indicate a change in emotional climate. Such expressions of feeling point to better relationships flourishing which cannot but affect the child positively. Whether the children could also be said to be demonstrating improved linguistic competence is a different question. If third party researchers use parental responses as an indicator of change, different results will emerge if the focus is on attitude or on linguistic gains. Focusing on areas of skill rather than on qualities of relationship reasserts the power of age norms to deflate parents. Valuable inter-personal gains pale as age norms parade deficits. If children are tested in their homes (however congenially) as a measure against which success will be later evaluated, onlooking parents inevitably imagine that the test items reflect significant things their children should know. They form expectations of what their child will be taught. They can then seek to remedy deficits by drilling concepts of size, shape, number, etc. The relationship can then deteriorate under pressurising anxiety. If expectations of the expert fix or miracle cure are engendered, parental engagement in a joint enterprise can diminish. Parents can pass their child over to the experts, or take on the remedial teacher role.

This brings us back to the parental agitation so commonly found in the wake of assessors in the home and shown in the opening narrative. Anxious parents, like the one described in the opening conversation, can also spend time parading their child's cleverness because they are dissatisfied by the measures of ability against which their children have been found to be lacking!

Establishing ease

On my first meeting at home, I seek to establish a rapport with the child and family and secure their full-hearted backing and collaboration. While ready to address parental concerns, I am mindful of conversation overheard by children of a worrying or disparaging kind and so attempt to leave painful developmental histories out of earshot of the child. The child needs to know where I fit in and so I give a flavour of the nursery sessions, highlighting favourites like sand, water, trains, jigsaws for the child's benefit. We play with toys which will be recognised later in the nursery and the child is at liberty to share with me favourite books or puzzles at home. Children fearful of separating from their parents, who go mute with strangers, need to trust those who will be working with them and parents need to entrust their children into caring hands. If the child will sit with me and share a book while mother goes out of the room on some pretext – to make a cup of tea for instance – the beginning of a trusting relationship is made. If I can join with children who have already been marked as troublesome and mutual liking is seen by parents, hopefulness about the 'new nursery' wells up. Parents need reassurance that their children will be accepted and at ease. They want to check out where their child is going and to be informed of the part they can play. That first visit seeks to include them in the play partner ethos. Helpful interactions are modelled and testing models avoided. So frequently, a meeting begun in agitation ends in relaxed laughter and marks the start of the joint process towards improvement. Parents are then more likely to transmit positive feelings to their children and to opt into the weekly parent sessions.

Preparing the ground for joint working contributes to the success of a short-term intervention and cannot sensibly be forgone. I have been told years later, that parents remember those first visits strongly. They point out that they felt able to hand over their precious children with confidence. They remember how hearing positive comments about their child brought tears to their eyes, when they were braced and on the defensive against bad news revealed by the 'assessment'. They were relieved to chase away the spectre of 'abnormality'. They remember how well their child 'took to you' and how they started to look forward to rather than to dread the 'new nursery'.

The dialogic alternative for parents

When they arrive, their first session introduces them to the conversational basis of language learning, the dialogic alternative. In pairs, parents practise listening and talking, two minutes in each role. Experientially, they see that communication requires looking and listening, remembering and responding, thinking what to say and actually coming out with it, taking turns and changing course. They feel the stress of being put on the spot, of having to talk to order. They feel the relief of being heard and of releasing bottled-up feelings. They sense the disruptive nature of some questioning and interrupting. They realise what a complex business it is and how subject to context and comfort the flow of conversation is. They can see where in the process their children are faltering and feel for them. They see why different children are 'in the same boat'. The eight children are seen to have different strengths and needs, yet they are all likely to be frustrated in their attempts to communicate. It is no longer a question of who is the worst! Negative behaviours like screeching or growling are seen as signals of this frustration, and it is reassuring to learn that difficult behaviour is commonplace in these circumstances. Such insights can take away the pressing need for a diagnostic explanation and direct energy into making changes that make sense. This is not about false reassurances or simple panaceas, nor is it about trying to fathom out what the experts mean; it's about facing painful knowledge, and feeling ready to do something straight away to help.

<hr />

Conversation with Bev Wilson, our researcher

Now that Bev Wilson, the researcher, is a practitioner of some years' standing, she has refined her view about the empirical paradigm and its usefulness in generating therapeutic outcomes. As a practitioner with several years of experience, she would proceed differently to judge benefits and ask different questions. Before, she was simply working within the paradigm favoured by her university, unaware of other ways of evaluating interventions. She was naturally primarily concerned to pass her degree. She had little experience of working with children to inform her method.

She felt that it would be helpful for trainee speech and language therapists to read this chapter so as to break away from a purely linguistic view within a medical model. She sees the importance of communication including interactions of a non-verbal as well as a verbal kind.

She has found that her working with groups of parents, on a Hanen programme with its slogan: 'It takes two to talk' (Manolson 1992), has come to be the most valuable part of her work as a speech and language therapist. She witnesses changes in children's readiness and ability to communicate, which far exceed the dubious gains of weekly clinic sessions. She listens to parents' comments on significant changes. She knows that it works to involve parents as communication partners and that parents have a long-term and intense commitment, which no professional has the time to match. If they are empowered and supported, their children will benefit.

Conversation with Judy Waters about her 'Let's Play' guide to interactive assessment

Judy Waters explained how she had started by considering the nature of play and seeking to 'validate' its use in interactive assessment. Dynamic assessment provided her with a useful framework, opening the way to considering the child's thinking and inter-action style as legitimate domains. She feels that dynamic assessment has helped 'to break the mould' of traditional assessment with its restricted view of 'what a child can do with materials in a particular way with a particular script'. She is more interested, however, in the play application and seeing 'how a child interacts and how that impacts' on her way of interacting with the child. She wants to explore what sort of 'conversa-tion' can emerge in what circumstances.

I asked her what sort of toys has she found to be especially useful. She said that the original set of things in her Bunny Bag were familiar to her. Because she had used them frequently, they had become a 'kind of reference point'. She advises people to include toys they are comfortable with. Her thinking about this has evolved: she used to choose items which could reveal a child's concepts, but increasingly, she is adding things like soap bubbles, pop-up toys, or marble runs to attract joint interest. She used to start with symbolic playthings, like teddy and teacups, but realised that for some children these presented too big a challenge to communicate. Instead, a jigsaw or shape-sorter might allow the child a successful arena to venture an interaction. She would save, until later, the more directly interactive toys or games. It is important to be flexible and to respond to the demands of the situation. The demands on assessment are often multiple, so it is good to have a range of possibilities available. If you only have a short time, it is better to 'get the quality of the interaction going' and return later to further the assessment.

She has learned from speech and language therapists to 'take time to look at where the child is and what interests him, and join the child there'. She has found that 'the best assessments give the child a bit of space'. The wonder of play assessment is that it is positive and enjoyable. You are respecting how the child plays, even when it may be very different from someone else's way of playing and thinking. You are not introducing alien items which are not part of the child's world. Too often, we as assessors are so pressed for time and so intent on getting through our preconceived agenda, that we 'deny our-selves the opportunity to explore the child's focus of interest and to find out what works to engage him'. If engagement is not the starting point, attempts to gauge a child's cog-nitive functioning can fail, because the child is put off. This creates 'assessment failures'. The following conversational extract cautions against assuming the failure lies in a child's inability:

> *Judy: So what you really need is an assessment paradigm (or whatever the word is) that's completely wide open. It allows you to explore what the child's giving you. If what the child's giving you is his back (and that happens sometimes too), then the task of the assessment is to find out what it takes for the child to give you a glance, or turn to face you, or take an interest in you, or in a thing. That is the assessment. That's what the assessment is about, because if it then becomes thing-based or*

item-based, you're not going to get anywhere, because all you're going to get is the back! So it's actually having the ability to say that it is valid to spend half an hour with the child exploring an interaction. I think that involves looking at assessment with completely new eyes.

Fleur: Twice now you've used the word valid and I think that this may be because of voices suggesting that it's not.

Judy: Oh yeah, you bet, it comes up all the time when I give the talks around the country. It almost always comes up at some point: how do you validate this?; it doesn't have a score; how do you do inter-user reliability? So many questions arise that are associated with validity, and people then start thinking about doing dynamic assessment with increased levels . . .

Fleur: So you can measure it?

Judy: So you can measure it. It's alien thinking to me. I try to connect with that but usually what I'm saying is: I'm trying to find something that works in that setting for me that enables me to make a hypothesis that might be useful to somebody else. It's a hypothesis, but it's something; it's not nothing; it's not the child's back facing me through the assessment. All we're doing in assessment is generating hypotheses. There are assumptions that a child's response has validity, but in fact I would say, 'Be humble about any assessment; it's only what's happened in one setting with one child and one person'. If it generates something that's more than a hypothesis, I'm immediately suspicious of it.

Fleur: Right, I feel exactly that: it's constantly generating a hypothesis which some-body else might be able to build on, and if that's as much as can reasonably be gen-erated, it doesn't make it worthless.

Judy: No that's right . . . So if you present a child with a task from the British Ability Scales, for example, and he does not do that task, or score on that task, it can only really be a hypothesis that the child is unable (given that set of circum-stances) to access that task. It's a far greater hypothesis to say that the child has not got that concept. It worries me hugely that in some clinical settings we're looking at scores on these standardised assessments and we're quoting them and we're saying that these give us information about a child when they may not. They may be completely invalid. Access to a set of materials and to a way of working with a person is the very first step. You can't miss out the access bit. Unless you're abso-lutely sure you've got the interaction going and the child is with you on a task, you can't really then go and quote the outcome of the task as something valid.

So it's a different way of thinking about assessment and what's going on in the assessment. Sometimes you have to work for that interaction. The actual access to materials is a goal really.

We wondered how this new way could be acquired. How does one become an interac-tive specialist, able to generate these kinds of hypotheses: how to approach, engage and enable new learning? Guidelines could be adopted, but applied in a mechanical, non-interactive way. It is difficult to get across those key qualities of curiosity and enjoyment of shared experience, the pleasure of that first look or move to communicate; that back just turning slightly.

Judy suggested that perhaps we needed to help people go in with a different set of questions and maybe we needed to make it simpler. It's so much simpler and more human to go and *be with* a child. Perhaps, sometimes, it's about 'giving permission for that to be a valid thing to do'.

Box 3.2 The Mediated Learning Experience (MLE)

1. **To help the child feel at ease (affective involvement)**

2. **To focus the child on task (mediation of intent)**
   Calling child's name
   Auditory stimulus (rattling the toy or choosing one which makes an interesting noise)
   Visual stimulus (moving the toy across the child's line of vision, choosing a visually interesting toy)
   Containment e.g. placing child on lap (with parental permission), placing the child on a chair close to table
   Use of voice (louder voice than usual, lots of expression)
   Maintenance of eye contact

3. **To focus attention on relevant features of the task (mediation of meaning)**
   Hand over hand assistance
   Demonstration (to maintain child's attention – this can be an elaborate mime, can be done by teddy etc.)
   Gesture (pointing to relevant aspects of the toy)

4. **To assist generalisation (transcendence)**
   Presentation of toys making similar cognitive demands

5. **To focus on assessor's role (mediation of joint regard/sharing behaviour)**
   Demonstration of trying and failing at task with appropriate expressions of sadness/frustration. Encouragement of child to help you solve the problem.

Taking turns
Modelling the task in parallel to the child (requires two sets of equipment)

6. **To help the child plan (task regulation)**
Non verbal demonstration of planning e.g. lining up nesting beakers in size order

7. **To help the child break the task down (mediation of psychological differentiation)**
Small parts or connecting aspects of the task can be presented one at a time and the child encouraged (possibly through demonstration) to do the task this way
Ensuring that the child him- or herself does the task, not the adult

8. **To help the child feel successful (mediation of feelings of competence)**
Starting with items below the child's abilities
Lots of praise for positive response
With more verbal children it can be helpful to ask 'how did you do that?'

9. **To help the child feel a sense of progress (mediation of challenge and change)**
With less verbal children this can be done via praise but this may not always result in a feeling of competence. With more verbal children it is important to interpret to them the fact that they have learnt a skill which was 'hard' to do and that they can do other ' hard' things.

Source: Judy Waters' *Guide to Mediation With Young Children* (1999), which takes 9 from the 11 mediated interactions of Feuerstein (1979) for use with young children.

CHAPTER 4

Counting Communication: An Observational Approach to Evaluation

I watched this little one as happy as a sandboy in the home corner, loading the washing machine, turning the knobs, doing the ironing. He knew exactly what to do in this domestic world and his teachers commented on his lovely symbolic play. He would play in the home corner all day every day if he had the chance. I was observing the other children coming in and out and all went well until one boy tried to snatch the box of soap powder from him. At first he allowed himself to be pushed and then you could see it in his face — a look which said, 'I can't stand for this' and I saw him stand full square, his feet apart, stretching as tall as he possibly could and he sort of clenched his hands up and snatched the box back and carried on. He won that battle.

I used to say to everybody, put yourself in the child's shoes. That is the only way to know what the child is thinking, feeling, and a good way to find out how to plan what needs to be done next, the next achievable goal.

(Sheila Liddle in conversation, November 2000)

This chapter arises from my joint working and conversations with Sheila Liddle, a retired teacher of pre-school children with communication difficulties in a specialised setting. She and I have collaborated on this chapter to ensure that my version of her study meets with her approval. As a reflective practitioner, she was concerned to evaluate her work and to operate in the spirit of action research to improve practice. There follows an account of her observational approach to assessment and intervention with these children. When she later took on the role of researcher, she refined the expertise she already had as a teacher committed to watching children closely. The Sentence Record (Figure 4.1a and b) was kept by anyone in the working team, and this preserved the narrative context so that the full meaning of a child's utterance could be reassembled and reflected upon later. Such observational assessments enabled the team to act directly in mediating more successful outcomes. There was a seamless line between assessment and intervention: the sense of the event from the child's viewpoint could be constructed and a helpful individual plan of action created.

For research purposes, she devised a method of counting the communication events she observed in nurseries and extracted a score, which allowed comparison to be made

SENTENCE RECORD: Re John

Sentence	Date first used	To whom (or to what) was it used?	What was going on?	What do you think he/she was trying to say?
Got brush	26/9/9–	SL	Picking up the tiny rake from the playmobile	I've got a brush
I not	9/10/9–	SL	He was going to cut his playdough ginger bread man's head then changed his mind!	I won't
Watch the tele Oh two tele Yes, I do it	11/10/9– 11/10/9– 6/11/9–	SL SL SL	Going to sit on the settee When I went to sit beside him On the settee I said I didn't know who had pinched all the pencils	Yes, I did
And that one . . . is in a knot John's finished this one	21/11/9– 6/12/9–	SL SL	Pointing to his other shoe lace while I unfastened one . . . John finished his jigsaw	
No water in there	12/1/9–		Pointing to the empty bowl	
Where's the top?	12/1/9–	SL	Looking for the kettle lid	
He's opened the door, self	12/1/9–	SL	When child came into the classroom	He's opened the door by himself
It won't go under	4/3/9–		Putting a bridge shaped brick over the railway track – estimating that the train wouldn't fit under	The train wouldn't go under
No black circles again	4/3/9–	NN	Register time – everyone here	

Figure 4.1a   Sentence record

OBSERVATIONS: Week 4–8 December 199–

Social Interactive	Play
	Still going to house by herself. Goes to baskets, holds up items. 'What's this?' She brought me the melon (whole), said 'pumpkin'. Remembered from Halloween. Very little interactive play with other chd, if any. Spotted new microwave & playing with it, turning knob etc. as with real one.
Cognitive	Motor
Has come 2x to watch me working with another chd. On mat with colours (bricks). Joins in a little, but soon loses interest even tho' she is included and moves away. Needs 1:1 then builds up a pair. Counts well to 10. Counts pictures one by one.	Absolutely *loves* music & singing. Little face lights up. We had music and movement in classroom this week with keyboard and she thoroughly enjoyed it. Beautifully neat, coordinated movements for dancing, rolling etc.
Receptive language	Expressive language
Looking very lost a lot of time when change of routine/ outing etc. Lots of 'why? why?' Unable to follow story, even when there are pictures. Loses interest and turns away – or comes out & drops pictures behind shelf as if she doesn't like feeling confused.	Lang. progressing when commenting on the 'here and now' – what's happening then.
Creative	Other
Still enjoying sand/water/paint most.	Still opting out. Takes all chances to go to toilet. 'me want wee wee.' If that doesn't work 'want poo-poo' (more urgent!!) 'want to paint', 'want to play in the house'.

Figure 4.1b Observations

between contexts and types of activity. Slipping from the role of teacher participating in events to the observer recording the flow of interactions was not as difficult as it might seem. Because recording was part of normal practice for those children, they accepted her temporary disengagement from their play to do her writing. Children saw writing as part of the process and even asked at times for their words to be written down. The extent to which the children were involved is illustrated by a child taking up the recording role when teacher was called to the phone; the teacher returned to be given the page covered in the child's mark-making. All the data collected built up a whole picture of the child's strengths and stresses in communication. In addition, guided interviews with parents and teachers of the chosen children were carried out to complement her own views.

If children on entry to the project had been tested on static linguistic features and then retested at the end, the effectiveness of the 'medicine' would rest on such evidence. Time spent either assessing competencies or teaching the desired concepts would inevitably reduce the time for interacting conversationally with children and 'joining' with their concerns. If, on the other hand, conversational exchanges were observed, and counted as a measure of success, then efforts could wholeheartedly be directed at enabling such turn taking. To find such measures was the motive for the research described here.

The Liddle study

This research is valuable to our thinking because:

(a) It gives a methodology based on observation and counting of communication events.
(b) It allows for comparison of communicative scores in structured and informal situations, in the mainstream setting and the segregated one.

Observing and counting communication events

Observations of target children communicating in their mainstream nurseries and in their specialist provision were made. Verbatim quotations were recorded. For each child, two conditions were compared in each setting: a structured setting and an informal play session, both for equal lengths of time. A communication score was computed to allow for numerical comparison (see Table 4.1).

Table 4.1 Comparison of the communication scores (CS)* for each child in mainstream nursery and special nursery

Name	Mainstream nursery		Special nursery	
	Structured	Informal	Structured	Informal
Callum	100	55	125	76
Amie	161	66	239	194
Ruth	63	50	124	178
Robin	73	87	115	213
David	98	56	167	206
John	181	143	225	181
Jack	122	84	89	79
Peter	97	63	139	73
Michael	**105**	**184**	**300**	**140**
Martin	81	58	170	91
Tom	141	76	177	118

*Communication score $= \dfrac{\text{Events}}{\text{Time}} \times 100$

Both initiations and responses of children were counted as communicative events. Non-verbal initiations and responses such as facial expressions, signs, gestures, and body language were also counted. If an initiation was met by no response, this was noted but not counted as an event. Using the coding scheme adopted by the famous 'child-watching' study (Sylva *et al.* 1980), the target child (TC) was the focus and inter-actions with adults (A) and other children (C) were clearly mapped in a conversational frame with direction of flow shown (A–TC) to mark initiation (I) or response (R).

In addition, further aspects of the exchange were noted but not counted as commu-nication events: anti-social behaviours and pro-social moves. Situational awareness was considered of significance in reconstructing the qualitative nature of the communica-tive event. It was considered important to gather evidence of a child's ability to listen and watch and respond to happenings of concern in the environment. Noticing the arrival of a newcomer to the room or a change in routine or appearance could be classed as examples of such situational awareness. If a child went further, and fetched a chair for the newcomer or invited him to sit alongside by patting an empty chair next to her, these actions could be classed as pro-social ones. Definitions of these additional aspects are shown in Table 4.2 where tallies of such instances in the three situations were addi-tionally made (see also Table 4.3).

Table 4.2 Totals for social activity and awareness of target children in mainstream nursery and special nursery

	Pro-social		Anti-social		Situational awareness	
	Mainstream Nursery	Special Nursery	Mainstream Nursery	Special Nursery	Mainstream Nursery	Special Nursery
Callum	2	7	2	0	3	2
Amie	0	8	2	0	1	0
Ruth	7	17	5	2	2	7
Robin	0	1	1	0	6	2
David	2	7	24	3	2	2
John	0	1	3	4	3	1
Jack	1	7	11	0	3	5
Peter	11	13	17	3	5	5
Michael	6	3	3	1	2	2
Martin	6	7	1	0	5	1
Tom	4	13	12	0	6	1
Total	39	84	81	13	38	28

KEY:
Pro-social activities include:
Sharing. Showing care, concern for or interest in another child or adult. Helping of own volition. Being polite, e.g. saying 'please' or 'thank you'. Engaging listener's attention.

Anti-social activities include:
Not sharing. Grabbing. Pulling, pushing. Hitting, kicking, biting, Retaliation. Deliberate lack of response, ignoring. Inattention. Not joining in. Being distracted.

Examples of situational awareness include:
Anticipating another's need. Responding positively or appropriately to something or someone in the environment. Following routine.

Table 4.3 Social activity and awareness: structured and informal situations

NAME	Pro-social Mainstream Nursery Str.	Inf.	Pro-social Special Str.	Inf.	Anti-social Mainstream Nursery Str.	Inf.	Anti-social Special Str.	Inf.	Situational awareness Mainstream Nursery Str.	Inf.	Situational awareness Special Str.	Inf.
Callum	1	1	4	3	2					3	1	1
Amie			4	4	1	1				1		
Ruth	6	1	9	8	4	1	1	1		2	7	
Robin				1	1				3	3	1	1
David	2		4	3	16	8		3	1	1	1	1
John				1	2	1	1	3		3	1	
Jack		1	1	6	2	9			2	1	3	2
Peter	4	7	9	4	4	13	3		2	3	3	2
Michael	2	4	3		3			1		2	1	1
Martin	3	3	3	4		1			3	2		1
Tom	3	1	6	7	5	7			1	5		1
Structured	21		44		40		5		12		18	
Informal	18		40		41		8		26		10	
Total	39		84		81		13		38		28	

Analysing the events yielded information about the nature of the interactions. The purpose or function of the event was gleaned from studying the interactions themselves after the observations were made rather than from pre-determined categories, or event sampling.

Comparing formal and free conditions

The observational method opened up to view the experience of the children and how they fared in both settings under two conditions: structured and informal. Structured situations were adult-led or adult-guided activities. The informal situations were ' free-choice, child-directed activities' (Liddle 1999: 54). Sometimes an observation, which started out as informal, switched to structured once the transcript was analysed. Children might initiate an activity which would be developed and taken over by the adult. So, this was no simple distinction between free play (= informal) and teaching sessions (= structured activities).

Results showed that the target children communicated more in the structured settings in both the mainstream and segregated situations. They communicated little in free play situations in the mainstream, but engaged with others in the special setting somewhat more frequently. Analysis of the type of encounter in each case revealed that in the mainstream, adult interactions were predominantly to control and organise, whereas those in the special situation served to model utterances, expand meaning, and articulate inadequate or non-verbal attempts to communicate (see Table 4.4).

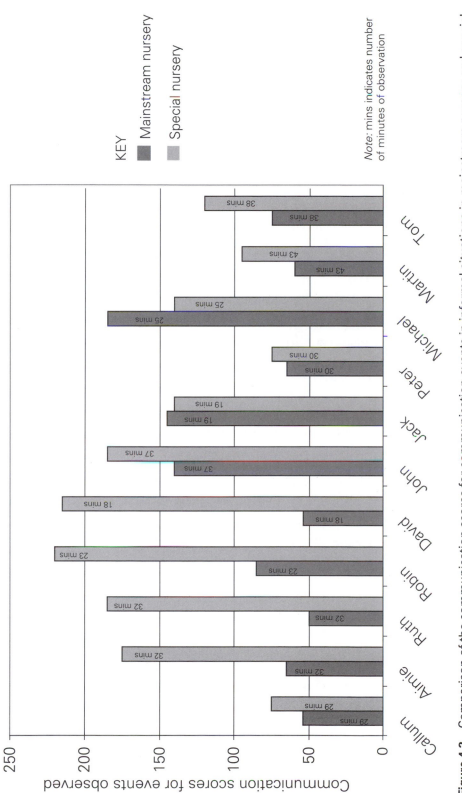

Figure 4.2 Comparison of the communication scores for communication events in informal situations in mainstream nursery and special nursery

Table 4.4 Total numbers of types of adult communication with target children

Type of A–TC communication event	Total no. in mainstream nurseries	Total no. in special nursery
Direction re task/activity	57	65
Question re task/activity	47	58
Comment re task/activity	16	16
Extending target child's utterance	1	12
Clarifying language for target child	1	16
Modelling speech/language	4	32
Responding to target child	24	72
Control of target child's behaviour	37	6
Praising or encouraging target child	10	39
Giving him/her support or reassurance	18	28
Greeting or saying 'Goodbye'	3	1

The observations of target children and interviews with their teachers and carers revealed similar findings to the Sylva *et al.* study (1980), which found little evidence of conversational exchange in nurseries and playgroups; it concluded that the image of the pre-school child involved in fantasy play with others or chatting away to a teacher rarely emerged in reality. The typical child was more likely to be seen 'Careering through the garden on a bicycle, blowing bubbles at the water table, or quietly watching another child paint' (Sylva *et al.* 1980: 81). Similarly, in the Liddle study, for large parts of the nursery day, children were seen to be wandering aimlessly or keeping a low profile with the same repetitive activities, particularly with sand, water and in the home corner. They neither sought out nor were found by adults, except to control/correct or push forward the organisation at tidy-up time. There was an attitude which avoided intervening unless the child showed an interest. Materials were laid out, but no adult modelled or mediated them unless the child first had a go with them.

The status afforded free play and misconceptions of child-centred approaches have bedevilled the early years arena. Research (Sylva *et al.* 1980) has exposed the paucity of ideas and lack of challenge that can attend nursery set-ups, which leave children to play uninterrupted for fear of spoiling their creative dramas. Also, the notion of the child as the solitary scientist exploring and learning by doing has arguably been responsible for much *laissez-faire* practice, and necessitated a call for skilled adult mediation.

This approach of leaving children to play without butting in contrasted with that of the segregated setting: there, the children were co-opted and led to join an activity. Children could not avoid adults even if they wanted to, and there were clear expectations that they take part and that they could expect to be helped and supported. Normal nursery procedures were followed albeit slowed down and expanded; no artificial drills or exercises were substituted or imposed. So, in effect there was not a gaping divide between play (left to your own devices) and work (activities organised by teacher with learning goals in mind). A link between participation and predictability was forged. Knowing the way juice time or weather time was run – what the adult was likely to ask and how picture support was used on a daily basis – meant that children could antici-pate how to join in and even find the confidence to take on the role of the adult. Here the operation of Vygotsky's 'zone of proximal development' was more than a high-sounding phrase; staff members were operating in that space, ripe for change, between the child's actual and potential levels of communication.

Accounting for results

An easy way to account for results would be simply to cite the beneficial effects of small numbers and of the expertise of the multi-professional team. This would inevitably lead to a clamouring for more segregated provision and give weight to exclusion as the way forward. A closer look reveals a more complex picture. What becomes apparent is the *inclusive* ethos of the segregated setting and the *exclusive* practices in many main-stream classes, however well meaning individual staff members might be. Pro-social encounters are the norm in the segregated setting. Here, the ethos is to welcome, to extol sharing, and to promote joint action, to engage in turn-taking and to articulate awareness of the needs of others. By contrast, contacts between peers in the main-stream are more often characterised by anti-social acts. There are instances of children calling on staff to take away the culprit, spoiling their game, or pushing aside the silent onlooker who has nothing to contribute. This difference, however, does not necessar-ily have to be the case. The exception in the data was a child named Michael. Unlike the other ten children in the sample, Michael interacted *more* frequently in informal situa-tions in his mainstream nursery than in the segregated setting, in spite of the usual pres-sures on staff time (see Figure 4.2). His story is therefore instructive. The rest of this chapter, therefore, digresses from the original study, in an attempt to probe possible reasons for this unrepresentative case. I use the Liddle observations and her interviews with Michael's teacher and mother as my sources. I had no direct contact with Michael.

Michael's story

The four observations (Box 4.1) immediately bring Michael alive and recreate the scene and circumstances in which he lives. Without knowing him, I can perceive the nature of his speech and language difficulties from reading these observations. I can pick up that he experiences difficulty coordinating both fine and large movements and I could infer that this includes managing the musculature that makes for speech. There are very few words clearly articulated, and when he talks away in a stream of sound, he is not understood. The context gives clues to his utterances as with 'poo' for shampoo' and 'bu' for 'bubbles' and his words are clear in intention if not in pronunciation, as in his attempts to tell about the 'snowman'. He is, however, very expressive in non-verbal ways. He uses signs, gestures, facial expressions and tones to get his message and needs across. He makes good eye contact, indicates a wish to play, joins in jokes, nods agree-ment and resists wrong interpretations. He is co-opted by other children (even when they do not understand him) into their play, because he responds to requests and initi-ates pretend sequences himself. He is ready with social smiles and nods and is aware of

Box 4.1 Michael in structured mainstream nursery 10.3.9–

KEY: NN   Nursery nurse   SALT   Speech and language therapist
       O   Observer   T   Teacher

10.10 a.m.   Michael has taken the observer to a table where three girls are playing a lotto game. He wants to join in, but will not do so unless the observer joins in too. The NN sees O's predicament (she needs to observe Michael) and sits down with Michael and the three girls. Michael is reluctant for observer to move away but she tells him she has jobs to do.

The NN gives the four children a board each. She holds up the first picture. Michael looks at it and at his board. (His movements are very slow.) Before he has finished looking a girl claims it. She puts it on her board. Michael is still looking for the first picture on his board when the next one is held up.

NN to Michael:	'Michael' to get his attention. It is one of his. He doesn't make any sound but looks again at his board then holds his hand out to take the picture, very slowly.
NN to Michael:	'It's a kite, isn't it Michael?' Michael does not reply. He is now trying to place his picture but again his motor difficulties affect him.
Emma to Michael:	'Put it this way Michael', as she helps him. Michael puts his hands on his lap and lets her do it. The game is continuing. He looks sometimes but is behind the other children in his reactions. They are beginning to lose concentration. When it is his picture next he says 'ball'.
NN to Michael:	'Ball', putting the picture on the table near Michael who struggles to pick it up. He takes two hands to it. He knows where it has to go and is concentrating on trying to place it while the game continues. He is unable to follow the verbal exchanges and interaction between the children and NN whilst he is trying to cope with the motor demands of the activity. NN does not hurry him but it is difficult to keep the momentum going. Emma has lost interest in him. He places his picture to his satisfaction and looks up at NN. The picture is a dog. He likes dogs. He looks at the board of the child opposite but there is no dog there. He is still looking when Lauren calls 'That's my dog.'
NN to Michael:	'Have you got a dog at home Michael?' (She knows he has.)

Michael nods to NN.

| NN to Michael: | 'What's he called?' |

Michael replies but it is unintelligible.

| NN to Michael: | 'That's a nice name.' |
| Mandy to NN: | 'I haven't got a dog but I've got a rabbit and a guinea pig. My auntie's got a big dog. It's an alsatian and it's called Rover.' |

Michael has turned away, he has lost interest.

The teacher calls that it is time to put the toys away for milk. Without waiting for NN to give instructions Michael pushes his board towards the middle of the table and gets up to leave.

| NN to Michael: | 'Just a minute Michael, let's put all the pictures away tidily.' He is not interested and makes minimal effort whilst the three girls collect them up. Michael is looking towards the mat area where the teacher is getting milk ready.   10.20 a.m. |

11.01 a.m.   The children are in the small room for story. Michael is sitting at the back to the side. The teacher is talking about coughs and colds. Michael is looking at her and listening. He vocalises. She calls children's names for the register. They are to answer 'Here I am' when their names are called. Michael is playing with his shoe-laces, but looks up at his name.

| Michael to T: | 'Ho yam' (for 'Here I am'). There is no reaction from teacher or children to suggest that Michael has said anything out of the ordinary. It is accepted without comment and treated in the same way as other children's replies. |

Michael is settled quietly ready for story as are the other children. The observer tells T she will have to go now and thanks her. Michael is looking at O and listening.

| O to Michael: | 'I'll have to go now. I'll see you this afternoon.' |

Michael nods. O watches from outside. The story is 'Peace at last'. Michael sits well, listening.

T speaks slowly and clearly, holding the book up and pointing to the pictures where appropriate. When she yawns Michael yawns. He makes a noise for snoring. By the time Daddy bear goes into the garden to try and get some sleep Michael is tired and loses concentration. He begins to look away and plays with his shoe-laces. He is not attempting to distract others but is not involved. 11.13 a.m.

Michael in unstructured mainstream nursery

10.35 a.m.   Michael says 'Hello' into the telephone in the house play area.

Boy[1] to Michael: 'Michael, will you put the washing in please.'

Michael goes to push the clothes into the washer.

Boy[1] to Michael: 'Thank you.'
Boy[1] to Michael: 'We need the powder in now.'

Michael pretends to put powder in and sets the controls again.

Boy[1] to Michael: 'I'll just do it again.' He laughs. He is teasing.

Boy[1] drops a pan. Teacher is walking by.

T to Michael: 'He's spilt the beans Michael', joining in the fun.

Michael gets another pan and upsets it, laughing.

Boy[1] to Michael: 'Oh Michael, you've spilt some more beans!'

Michael goes to get a cloth. There is lots of laughter as he pretends to wipe up. He puts the cloth back and sets the washing machine again.

Boy[2] to Michael: 'Michael, why do you turn that?' Michael turns towards the boy with good eye contact, Michael smiles and vocalises.
Boy[2] to Boy[1]:   'What's he saying?'
Boy[1] to Boy[2]:   'I don't know.'

Boy[3] comes into house area. He puts all the clothes back in the washer and shuts the door. He tries to stop Michael putting washing powder in. Michael pulls the washing powder away from Boy[3], vocalising firmly.

Boy[3] to Michael: 'Give it to me, I'll do it.'

Michael succeeds in holding on to the packet. He opens the washer door and pretends to put powder in.

Boy[3] to Michael: 'Put it back on the window sill', taking the packet when Michael puts it down.

Michael looks at Boy[3] and walks away, ignoring the instruction. He goes to the telephone, opens a book (diary or book of messages?) and 'writes' in it. He says 'hello' on the telephone. It falls and Michael vocalises at length as he tries to pick it up and put it straight.

Michael goes to the draining board where Boy[3] has been washing up.

Boy[3] to Michael:	'I need a drying (for 'frying') pan.' Michael is holding the frying pan. Boy[3] tries to take it from him but Michael pulls it away and puts it on the cooker with a spoon in.

Boy[3] retreats and sits at the table.

Boy[3] to Michael:	'It's breaksast (for 'breakfast') time.'

Michael continues to stir his frying pan.

A man comes into the nursery, a workman. Michael turns to see when he hears him talking to the teacher. A girl comes into the house area. Michael leans forward and shouts at her, she has taken the teapot out of the house. She comes back and takes the bucket.

Girl to Michael:	'It's ready.' Michael puts a bowl into the oven.
Girl to Michael:	'No, off, it's my bowl.' She comes to the oven and tries to open the door. She is holding her bucket with oven gloves.
Girl to Michael:	'Hot.' She wants to transfer the 'hot' pretend contents of her bucket to the bowl.
Girl to Michael:	'Just cooking', as Michael watches her. She tries to take the pan he is using. He grabs it quickly and puts it away in the cupboard, on the stacker with the others.

Another girl comes in.

Girl[2] to Michael:	'I'll do the sweeping up', as she takes the dustpan and brush and sweeps the floor round his feet. He has two girls to contend with now! He drops his hands to his sides and lets the girl sweep. Then he lifts up the brim of her hat and smiles at her.
Girl[2] to Michael:	'Michael, that's not funny', crossly. (She knows he is trying to sabotage her sweeping!)

Michael moves quietly away leaving the girl with the oven gloves tidying up. The sweeper has gone to sweep elsewhere. He goes to get some paper and a pencil and comes to sit beside the observer mark making, watching and listening to Girl[2] and another who are playing with the telephone.

Michael posts his letter in the post box.

Michael to O:	'You', and he points to the chair beside him. Plates crash in the house and he turns.
Michael to O:	'Arr' as if to say 'Oh dear'. He posts another letter, vocalising as he does so. He picks up a book and holds his pencil ready. The teacher has just come along.

T to Michael:	'Oh don't write in there sweetheart.' He immediately puts the pencil down. He 'reads' the book for a moment and then posts it!
T to Michael:	'You've posted the book!' Michael smiles, turns the post box round and pats it as if to say 'There's a book in there'.
Michael to T:	'For you' (attempted), as he passes her the 'phone.
T to Michael:	'She wants to talk to you Michael', listening then holding it towards Michael.

Michael takes the 'phone, 'talks' into it then says clearly 'Bye mam'.

He goes by himself to the playdough and comes back to observer with a cake tin and some playdough.

O to Michael:	'Oh, take it over to the playdough table.' He does. Teacher goes to tidy and Michael helps.
T to Michael:	'Put the rolling pin in there Michael', passing him a tin. He does. He tidies up more playdough then comes to the observer.
Michael to O:	'Story' (attempted), as he points to the story room. He takes O's hand to lead her in with him. 11 a.m.
O to Michael:	'Oh, I have to go soon.' His face falls. He stands with her as she writes then gestures to her to go in with him.

Michael in structured special nursery 1.3.9–

1.05 p.m.   Michael has taken his seat ready for 'picture time' (day/weather). T calls the register. Children to answer or attempt 'Yes' or 'Yes . . .', with teacher's name if they can. Non-verbal children to nod. Michael attempts 'Yes'. When teacher has finished Michael points up to the top of the cupboard where the register and pens are kept out of the way. She reaches up on her tiptoes and Michael smiles. While she is putting the register up there Michael picks up the bag with the pictures in and sits down on the teacher's chair. He begins to sort and separate the pictures from each other.

T to Michael:	'You're going to be teacher today are you, Michael? Off you go then', and she goes to sit on the chair he vacated. The children have gone quiet and are waiting, looking at Michael. He takes up the children's picture cards. Each child has previously selected a picture to represent them. Michael looks at the first, a bee, and waves it towards the appropriate child with vocalisation.
Child to Michael:	'Ta' (for 'thank you'), taking the picture.

Michael repeats this with the other six children. He knows who has each picture. He puts his own down beside him with a laugh. The task is confidently done and the children wait patiently.

T to Michael:	'Well, that was really good Michael. Well done.' She claps and the children join in.

Michael gives a big smile and gets up to return to his chair.

T to all:	'Which picture do we need today?' as she looks at the weather pictures.

Michael does the action for 'cold'. Martin chooses the cold picture and puts in on the board. The teacher begins to sing the song for a cold day. 'This is the way we put on our hat . . . on a cold and frosty afternoon', Michael joins in the singing in his own way and does the action for 'hat' and for 'cold' at the appropriate time.

T to all:	'What do we put on next?'
Jack to T	'Coat.'
T to all:	'Have you got a zip or buttons? I've got buttons today.' She sings the verse with the children joining in, doing the action for fastening buttons. Michael does a zip action. Scarf next, then gloves. Michael does the actions, still singing, and lastly . . .
T to all:	'And what keeps our feet warm?'
Chorus of 'Boots'.	They sing 'This is the way we put on our boots . . .' Michael pretends to pull his boots on.
T to all:	'Oo, I'm lovely and warm now. Are you?' Michael nods. 1.13 p.m.

Note: This is a routine sequence which can be varied from day to day to last as long as is wished. Where children want to take over the adult's role they are encouraged. Michael shows awareness of his motor slowness by organising the taking hold of each picture in advance.

1.16 p.m.   'Talking time'. Looking at 'Silly pictures' (What's wrong?) Five boys with NN.

NN holds up picture of boy drinking soup with a fork. She waits for children's reactions.

Peter to NN:	'Dinner'
Michael to NN:	'Wor' (for 'fork')
NN to Michael & Peter:	'That's right. He can't drink soup with a fork. He needs a spoon.'

NN holds a picture of baby sitting in the pet's basket.

Michael to NN:	'Ta' (for 'cat')
NN to Michael:	'Good boy. Baby can't sit in there. It's a cat's basket, or the dog's basket.'

NN holds up a picture of a girl brushing her hair with a long handled sweeping brush.

Martin to NN:	'Rub it away.'
Michael to NN:	'Dust pan'
NN to children:	'Yes, silly girl. She can't brush her hair with a sweeping brush.'
Martin to NN:	'Me don't.'
NN to all:	'What does she do with the big brush?'
Martin to NN:	'Oh oh, sweep the floor.'
Peter to NN:	'Me that bigger one', pointing to the long handled brush in the picture and meaning 'I use that for sweeping the floor'.

The next picture is a girl eating a sandwich with a flower in it.

Peter to NN:	'That one', pointing to the flower.
Tom to NN:	'Flower'
NN to Tom:	'Do you eat a flower in your sandwich?'
Tom to NN:	'No'

Michael shakes his head and laughs.

Kevin to NN:	'Not me.'

The next picture is the man going to work. He is dressed except for his trousers. (His boxer shorts are white with blue spots.)

Tom to NN:	'Trousers, he naughty.'
NN to children:	'That's right. Silly man, he's forgotten to put his trousers on. Look at his knobbly knees' (laughing)
Peter to NN:	'My daddy are' with a shake of his head (meaning 'My daddy's knees aren't knobbly.'
Kevin to NN:	'Umbrella stick' (the man is carrying his umbrella like a walking stick).
Michael to Kevin:	'Rain'

NN holds up picture of a boy playing football with a cauliflower.

Peter to NN:	'Ball'
Kevin to NN:	'A concungcung' (for 'cauliflower')
NN to all:	'That's right. Silly boy. Go and get the ball you silly boy. Mammy will be cross. She cooks the cauliflower, in the pan, for dinner doesn't she?' 1.24 p.m.

Note: The NN in this observation was helping in the absence of the regular NN. There would usually have been more follow up of children's utterances to draw further discussion and bring out the humour of the pictures, for example what does go into sandwiches (the adult could say 'I like ham best in my sandwiches') and having fun about what colour underwear dads like. The use of a spoon to drink the soup would more likely have been drawn from the children rather than given to them. Nevertheless it was a useful session and the children responded well. This is a more demanding type of language activity and while the confidence and skill levels of the children are limited too much pressure is best avoided.

2.30 p.m.   Milk time

Michael is washing his hands ready for fruit and milk. He says 'hot' and 'cold' appropriately, turning to the teacher who is supervising. He pulls two paper towels from the dispenser, keeping one and passing the other to Martin. He is thoughtful while drying his hands. He puts the wet towel in the bin, turns and walks into the classroom. SALT is ready at the table, holding the plate with a banana and an apple.

Michael to SALT:	'My round?' (for 'Can I take it round?')
SALT to Michael:	'Well you did the pictures today, didn't you Michael? We'll let someone else take the fruit round.'
Martin to NN:	'Me take it round', sitting up very straight.

SALT prepares the banana for the children to pull a section of skin off each, in turn. Michael is slow to take the skin between finger and thumb but pulls firmly once he has hold.

SALT to Michael:	'Michael pull' as he does so. She cuts the banana into pieces. Marie takes it round and puts an extra piece in her mouth as she does so. Michael sees her. He draws his breath in, looks at the adult, shakes his head and puts one finger up.
SALT to Michael:	'Yes, we saw that didn't we Michael? One piece of banana each. Well, Marie can't have any apple, what a shame.' (Marie has done this a number of times and this is the management procedure now.)

Michael looks at Marie as she sits down. She stamps her feet and hits the table when Martin takes the plate with apple past her, but no one takes any notice.

Michael to Martin:	'Ta' (saying 'thank you' for his apple)
Michael to SALT:	'Baby soft play' (meaning 'The babies are in soft play')
SALT to Michael:	'No, not today, We can go in.'

Michael puts his arms up and cheers.

SALT to Michael:	'After singing.' 2.36 p.m.

The NN asks the children what colour cup they would like. Michael points to the brown one. He says 'ta' when given his cup of milk and drinks it quickly. He finishes it and holds his cup out, then puts it down, raises himself up by pressing on the table with his hands and arms, takes hold of his cup again and stretches across to NN, in front of SALT.

SALT to Michael:	'My, you've drunk that quickly Michael. Would you like some more milk?'
Michael to SALT:	'Yes please' (attempted) with a nod.
SALT to Michael:	'Well just wait until everyone has finished.' He sits down again. 2.40 p.m.

Michael in unstructured special nursery

1.45 p.m.   Pretending to bath the doll in the house corner. He takes baby bath to sink and pretends to turn on the tap. 'Tests' the water and says 'hot'. He turns the tap off and goes to the table where he puts the bath down. Lots of sounds and vocalisation. Says 'baby', 'poo' as he reaches for the shampoo and 'bu' for bubbles as he pretends to wash doll's hair. He looks for a towel to dry doll's hair. He puts the doll wrapped in a towel on the bed and puts the blanket over her then puts his finger to his mouth and creeps away.

He finds a fork under the house play kitchen cupboard and takes it to show NN.

Michael to NN:	'Found a wor' (for 'fork')
NN to Michael:	'Oh, where did you find it?' Michael points towards the house corner and then does the action for 'under'.
NN to Michael:	Well done. Put it away in the box.' Michael takes it to the kitchen and puts it in the box, looking through the items inside before putting the box on the cupboard top. 1.55 p.m.
NN to all:	'Oo look everybody, it's snowing.' The children stop what they are doing and look towards the window. Snow is falling. They run to the window to look out, Michael included.
NN to all:	'It's very quiet, isn't it? You can't hear it, not like the rain.' Everyone is watching the snow falling.
NN to all:	'Do you think it's going to lie on the ground? I don't like driving in the snow. But we could make a snowman tomorrow.'
Michael to NN:	'Mam__? snowman__? home.' (About 5 words, probably about making a snowman with mam when he gets home).

There is great excitement.

NN to all:	'House is closed now everyone.' She has put the face up with the sad mouth which means not to play in the house corner. The happy face means the house is open. This is done to encourage the several children who tend to spend all or most of the time in the house area to explore other activities. Michael is one of these children.

Michael looks at the NN and goes straight to the bead threading. He threads with his left hand, standing up. He chooses bricks and beads which he threads with some success, apparently at random as there does not seem to be a pattern to colour or shape. He is more confident than he used to be with this activity. Peter wants his in a necklace. NN ties it for him and puts it round his neck.

Michael to NN:	'Mam' and signals round his neck too.
NN to Michael:	A necklace, like mammy's, Michael. I bet your mammy looks pretty when she goes out.'

Michael nods and smiles. NN fixes his necklace round him. Looking at Peter, Michael gestures towards the mirror with vocalisation. He and Peter go to look at themselves.

Michael moves on to the 'tap tap', the hammer and nails with wooden farm shapes and a cork board. He tries to hold the nail with his right hand (wrist up and forward, it looks rather awkward). He hammers first with his left hand then changes to left hand to put the nail in the board. This is better but he has a fine tremor. Good hitting on the nail head. He perseveres, concentrating hard. His movements are slow.

NN to Michael:	'Well done. Find the horse', as she passes the table. Michael looks at the shapes and finds it, picking it up with some difficulty.
Michael to NN:	'There.'
NN to Michael:	'Well done.'

Michael swaps hands again as he organises himself to hammer the nail through the small hole and pin the horse shape to the board. He moves away after this. Michael goes to NN. He points to the cupboard and does a hoovering action. 2.05 p.m.

NN to Michael:	'The hoover. Just for a little while Michael' and she gets the toy hoover out of the cupboard for him. (Again kept out of sight due to its popularity. The children fight over it.) Michael takes the suction plug and fixes it onto the table, then hoovers round the floor, vocalising and smiling.

Tom stands in the way and Michael pretends to hoover Tom's feet, they both laugh. After a while Jack goes to Michael.

Jack to Michael:	'My turn now', and he tries to take the hoover. Michael holds it and pushes Jack away. Jack looks towards the NN. She has seen the events.
NN to Jack and Michael:	'Come on you boys. You have one more hoover Michael then let Jack have a turn.' Michael pushes the hoover once round the table then pretends to switch it off at the side and passes it to Jack.
NN to Jack:	'What do you say Jack?'
Jack to Michael:	'Thank you.'
NN to Michael:	'Good lad, Michael.' Michael smiles. He goes over to the window to look out at the snow which has started again. 2.10 p.m.

A colour matching game using bricks is out on a table. The two girls are there. Michael joins them. He matches a yellow brick to the yellow square on his board, then a blue one to a blue square. He picks up the yellow thread with a yellow bobbin tied on, and threads four more yellow bobbins. He holds it up by the end of the thread and shakes it. It makes a loud rattling noise and he smiles and vocalises noisily.

Note: The end of this observation provides a good example of what can be gained for assessment of the child's ability levels from informal observation in a naturalistic situation.

newcomers and happenings around him. He happily joins in action songs and follows the routines of the nursery. Given the chance, he assumes the role of the teacher and manages the picture allocation task by action rather than by words. He clearly comprehends language and is inclined to be obedient when instructed by the teacher, responding to praise. He can take on board explanations that require him to be satisfied with one turn only or to share the much-prized hoover.

From this information, it would be possible to suggest some interventions. The nursery nurse was alert to Michael's wish to be included in a game of lotto, and with some adjustments this could be a satisfying activity for all the children. Michael would probably like to be the one to hold up the cards and with help speak their names. He might like to indicate a match by calling out, and have a friend to place the pictures for him. This way, his motor difficulties do not slow up his participation. Further chances for role reversal with visual prompts are likely to please him. Clearly helping him to join in action songs is indicated. Being a facilitative player in the home corner is another avenue with many possibilities. There is nothing particularly *special* about such interventions and in Michael's case, the mainstream situation was ensuring that he belonged and was not seen or treated as *different*.

This was conspicuous in the answers offered by the staff in the interview. Michael's teacher noted that he came to adults for comfort and reassurance. He would also come with them to try activities. If he were busy, he would decline with a shake of the head. Faced with refusal, most nursery staff would back off and leave children alone.

Significantly in this case staff said they would 'try and coax him and get round him somehow.' Also, Michael would initiate contact:

> Yes, he would frequently come across wanting to show us something, perhaps tell us something. There were odd words that we could pick up on as we got used to listening to him. When we were able to understand, his face would light up and he would nod furiously as if to say 'Yes, yes, that's it'.

This one extract enshrines an enabling approach to the child. Efforts are channelled into understanding situations from the child's viewpoint. Everyone in the nursery is included in the 'we' of the extract above. He is not seen as a problem or in the category of expressive language disorder. His cooperation and participation are actively sought and engineered if necessary. Staff supervise and suggest rather than stand by as a resource. Of course, it could be said that Michael had personal qualities and abilities that prompted the treatment he received. He was non-verbally expressive and socially aware. He was quick to receive messages and self-confident enough to assert himself, as can be seen in the account at the beginning of the chapter. To explain his success thus would detract from the considerable efforts of this particular nursery to understand, engage and include Michael. Here is a case of the school ethos making a difference and of mainstream children modelling supportive behaviours of their teachers:

> Because you do try and create a caring environment, that maybe if a child is falling down, you would comfort that child . . . and you would see other children comforting that child. Similarly when Michael was upset, they would have seen us comforting Michael . . . you don't know whether it is sort of by example.

His teacher was at pains to emphasise that the children were aware that Michael did not speak and would ask about this, but that their attitude was concerned and 'protective', without 'babying' him. Children would seek out the adults to come and help or comfort him. Although his lack of expressive language meant he did not engage in cooperative play, he had a 'presence':

> He loved anything to do with domestic play . . . he would love loading the washing machine with clothes and he seemed to know exactly what to do . . . he obviously watched his mam and dad at home . . . he would shake the clothes and find places to drape them and he would follow through that kind of play . . . setting the table . . . and while Michael was doing that . . . there would be three or four other children sitting round the table chatting and Michael was doing his own thing . . . and there would be acknowledgement and smiles from Michael . . . he would tell them or indicate by tapping them to show them something . . .

He would involve himself in games of chase and his laughter was infectious. He was not 'intimidated' by boisterous companions, and 'seemed able to cope in handling himself quite well with a mixture of personalities'.

In the early days of Michael's attendance at nursery school, he could be very upset when his mother left and a member of staff was ready to distract him with a favourite story in a quiet place. This place was used for any child needing reassurance, and meant that everyone was not distressed by crying:

> *With whichever one of us took him from Mam, he would be reassured by a story. He seemed to need security of the routine . . . there would be a choice of four stories . . . one of the Spot stories . . . and after having that story usually in a little room away from the other children . . . he would then be quite happy to go and join the rest of the children and the activities.*

Michael's mother, also, has contributed to her son's happy inclusion. The interview with her revealed a daily pattern of mother and son playing and working alongside each other. The reason for his comfort in the house corner seemed to lie in his domestic partnership with his mother at home. As she ironed, he copied on his toy iron. He helped to load the washing machine and unpack and shelve the shopping. She stayed alongside Michael, and he helped her with the chores. She calmly attuned herself to his needs. She also provided an unpressured pace and accepting stance about his obvious difficulties. She inferred his meanings and read his replies, turn-taking, conversing and negotiating with him. There was a reciprocal quality to their interactions.

What can be taken from this research?

Most importantly, it underlines the need for evaluation to accord with the aims of the intervention. It focuses on communication events rather than on individual gains on linguistic measures and attempts to bring under scrutiny, the conditions and interactive quality of such dynamic events. Rich observational data allows for reconstruction of the situation after lapses in time and communicates more readily with other professionals and parents not present at the time. Documentation also leads straight to consideration of ways of engaging the child, using strengths and emerging competence in communication (verbal and non-verbal) as a basis. It allows the team of staff to reflect and plan and not wait on external data and advice to implement strategies.

It discusses teacher approaches and strategies for engaging in conversations and how to create inclusive communities. Findings prompt the query whether simply including children with communication difficulties alongside mainstream peers in the hope that they will 'catch' language from a rich culture can work. Very special adult mediation of language with such children is indicated if communication is to be initiated and sustained across conversational turns on topics of mutual interest. Finally, it throws light on the vexed question about the effect of structure on learning.

Conversations about structure

The question certainly vexed the conversationalists round my table. We agreed the concept of 'structure' needed deconstructing since its various interpretations led to dispute amongst practitioners. The concept of *drills* is sometimes aligned to 'structure' and brought up for some notions of mechanistic practices used in the interests of regimentation and conformity. Others thought of enabling and comforting *scaffolds* and supports to learning, as advocated by social constructivists (Bruner, Vygotsky). More neutral responses to the word equated 'structure' with *routines* and acknowledged the sense of security and control that knowing the ropes brought to all children, and particularly to children with communication difficulties. Following the same pattern each day allowed children to anticipate events and so be ready to participate in well-known scripts and enactions. Children loved the familiar, often preferring to recognise the old rather than be surprised by the new. There was nothing 'normal' about a nursery until routines and procedures created familiar ceremonies. The home corner, water play or sand tray linked with earlier experience of such things but learning how to 'play' in this context with many other children and few adults could be like completely new territory to negotiate. Specialised language nurseries set up the areas to be found in mainstream nurseries but provided a map: a visual timetable set out in pictures the order of events and children chose symbols of the play opportunities, which matched areas. Play partners (the adults involved) were at the ready to join and model so that the chances of turn taking dialogues around shared activity were exploited. They could be said to be structuring the 'free' situation and engaging in prototype conversations. Repeating the play sequences could become routines which were welcomed by the child. In a small group, songs and rhymes provided the repetition and taking turns to twinkle the star or run the mouse up the clock ensured participation. What was important was not simply the drill but the sense of belonging and ownership that came from being able to join the group dynamic. Initiating and taking roles, rather than passively passing by, were seen as the first step towards active communication.

CHAPTER 5

Mind the Gap

1: Between Theory and Practice

Even if we started with a child like Peter who was interested in diggers, and we introduced that into the pencil area and were drawing diggers and talking about roads and acting out little scenarios, making it into a social event, there would come a point in the morning when it was no longer appropriate to have conversations about diggers. Parents would expect to put a stop to it. It is hard knowing how much to allow and how much of the child's interest to use when it becomes the sole topic.

(Dorothy in conversation)

As our expertise and knowledge develop alongside other professionals', we are starting to see such behaviours (like hand-flapping) as a trigger or a cause or a communication which needs considering.

(Jill in conversation)

This central section attempts to transmit practical ideas and strategies to support pre-school children with communication difficulties. Many of the strategies are well known already and we have a book list available (Pourde 1989; Quick and O'Neal 1997; Rickerby and Lambert 1997; Sher 1995; Weber 1993; Weitzman 1992). Such transmission is not a simple passing on of the tricks of the trade. It inevitably deals in doubt and dilemma as well as in certainty about approaches as is seen by the opening conversation. The fruits of experience are hard won and often tacitly rather than explicitly known. We have been trying to make the tacit explicit in our reflections on practice (Polanyi 1967).

Our team of four (teacher, support teacher, speech and language therapist and educational psychologist) has conducted in-service training for interested professionals, and so we have had to think about how best to put across our methods. We wanted the sessions to be primarily practical and present opportunities for hands-on use of materials. Watching of illustrative videos and live demonstrations were of prime importance. The team has refined and altered its practice as a result of reflection and we have recently met together to record our reflections. So this chapter also includes some ideas on reflective practice and professional development.

Gaps between theory and practice

I have long been concerned by the gap that often opens up between experienced practitioners and academics. I have frequently been to conferences which drew hundreds of workers seeking support and ideas to guide practice with tricky 'cases' on Monday mornings. Faced with research data and methodological issues and problems of interpretation, these professionals often confessed to being 'lost' or 'bored' because there seemed little connection between research findings and their daily anxieties and dilemmas. On the other hand, researchers can be heard to lament that research knowledge is not being absorbed into improved practice. Some researchers note that it is difficult to beam in on everyday practice which has become unthinkingly automatic, because practitioners resist introspection, unless there is a crisis or a troubling jolt to the ordinary. For example, researchers investigating assessment practices for children with hearing impairment noted the following:

> Everyday professional practice includes much that has been overlearned, skills and perceptual judgements that have become habitual, and procedures that have been totally integrated into people's 'automatic' repertoires. Asking somebody to pay attention to these, now commonplace phenomena can easily appear intrusive. The inquiry may be seen as unnecessary or uninteresting. (Parlett 1991: 213)

By 'examining the details of practice' and 'opening up to closer inspection certain features of the everyday world of practice', it was hoped that 'the taken-for-granted' would once again become 'newsworthy', and critical consciousness would be raised 'with a view toward practical improvements' (ibid.: 214). What in this case was interpreted as resistance could equally be seen as lack of confidence and an undervaluing of considerable skill. Our team members started our evaluation session with the comment that 'we tend to undervalue our skills'.

Other researchers have revealed that there can be a gap between what practitioners profess to espouse by way of theory, and what they do in practice. For example, most nursery staff members profess the value of play to learning, but until they see themselves and the children in action on video, they are unaware of discrepancies. They can then query whether much learning is taking place when children are simply left to play. It appears that often 'the rhetoric of play is not realised in practice' (Bennett *et al.* 1997: 6). Exposing these gaps could be a sobering or deflating experience, so any reflective work needs to be carried out in a collaborative and supportive manner:

> An interpretative stance automatically connotes a co-operative approach since an understanding of participants' perspectives is not possible without extended interaction which in turn requires a common agenda, and a sympathetic and empathetic relationship between researcher and researched. In other words – research with, rather than research on teachers. (Bennett et al. 1997: 26)

Until such mismatches are exposed in an empathetic situation, it is difficult to embark on reflective consideration.

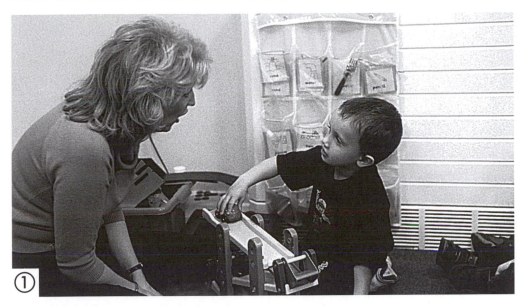

Listening and waiting for the 'Go!' before letting the car run.

He's sitting for longer. He's pointing to show you things and coming out with words without being prompted. He's listening and joining in with others and repeating the actions to the songs. He is so much more vocal. (Parent)

A shared moment of surprise at the craft table.

His confidence has gone through the roof. He's calling out, and coming out with words without thinking. There was no way he would have done that six weeks ago. I have adjusted my hopes: I did want to have a proper conversation with him, but I am very happy that he is no longer so quiet and withdrawn. (Parent)

Reflective considerations

We use video and photographs to stimulate discussion and reflection. To increase levels of awareness is a step beyond the SWOT analysis (*S*trengths, *W*eaknesses, *O*pportunities, and *T*hreats), that we undertook as a starting point.

The first observation made in our situation was about the change in our approach to playing with children over the past five years. We used to 'call children to us to carry out "games", rather formally to teach desired concepts'. We now question the usefulness of applying such a mixture of teaching and testing. Instead, we join with children's interests and develop stories and thus develop their language more incidentally. There is more sharing in the fun and surprise springing from play opportunities in the sand-tray and water play. Still, however, we can feel guilty at 'just playing' and feel the need to justify ourselves. The speech and language therapist, in particular, was concerned that her professional expertise was slipping while she was having 'fun', and she sometimes imagined a critical colleague judging her time spent in such play adversely since she was not specifically 'on target'. Yet she felt she was working in a context, which was the envy of most therapists: a non-clinical, educational setting familiar to the child. This 'naturalistic' setting she saw as a major asset for inducing language use. The team agreed that it was vital to keep our play-based approach and to maintain our staffing levels to allow for time to observe, record and discuss what to do next.

Sitting aside simply to observe and record also set off guilty feelings about wasting teaching time! Assigning a member of the team to observe and record would enhance the importance of the role. By documenting important breakthroughs in learning, the informal moment of value would not be lost. It was suggested that closer observations could reveal, for example, how children entered the home corner: their ways of announcing their arrival, addressing their companions or inviting joint attention. What about greetings, calling someone by name to look, giving and taking?

Pressures on time are always mentioned. Certainly time has been taken from intervention by an increase in formal testing in response to demands for statutory advice on increasingly more 'serious cases'. It was also less easy to note strengths for fear of weakening the case for providing additional resources.

Reflecting on photographs

By looking at two photo sequences of playful exchanges with children in our setting, it became apparent that the adult role was significantly different from regular nursery practice. Wearing a painting apron and painting alongside a child, on a shared piece of paper, was not something generally seen in mainstream nurseries. Rarely are adults seen in the water play or with dolls' house or farm animals. The photos also demonstrated the turn-taking quality of the 'conversation without words', the alternation of watching and doing by each member of the pair. The adult seems to be providing a friendly companion for children who would otherwise be solitary and largely silent as they sift sand or pour water. The photo sequence captures the shared emotions of surprise, joy, shock, suspense, etc. There is mutual regard and relationship.

Another interesting comment arose from the ordering of the sequence (see pp. 80 and 81). The most expressive moments, which you would expect to be the climax of a play sequence, were in fact the first picture in the series of negatives. This made us think that we often intervened in solitary play with a strong emotional reaction to attract attention. This was like the *Interrupt* of the Hanen programme (Manolson 1992), which one parent renamed *Irritate*, reminding us that intervening is a matter of tact and sensitivity! On the other hand, since play patterns can be repeated over and over again, it is difficult to judge which is the first picture in a cycle, and the most dramatic moment could be the one which first captured the photographer's gaze.

We felt happy about seizing the moment, capitalising on a lucky chance thrown up in play, but were aware that this could leave targets forgotten, and lesson/individual plans 'not ticked off'. It is difficult in this way to keep track of learning taking place, and to ensure that certain children do not miss out. We were also aware that forging 'fun' encounters with individuals in a small group with a good staff/child ratio was not seen as an option readily available to the ordinary nursery teacher in a full and busy classroom. It could, however, be the role of a teaching assistant.

Being conscious of our privilege, we aimed in our course to put across 'our philosophy by demonstration'. In this book, we hope that the photographs speak in our absence and illustrate strategies like the use of the visual timetable (photo 1, p. 87); of wait-time to gain good looking and listening (by ready-steady-go games, as in photos 1, p. 77 and 4, p. 88); of turn-taking patterns in play (photo 2, p. 87) with the *OWL*ing of the Hanen Programme (Manolson 1992, i.e. *O*bserve, *W*ait and *L*isten) and of emotional engagement with the child's interest (photos 2, p. 77 and 3, p. 88). A number of these 'discourse' features have been shown to affect the development of language in the early years (Ellis Weismer 2000). We were trying to put across *how* we interact with the children and so we were heartened to hear the following comments of course participants in the closing round:

> *I realise that working with such children does not need special equipment – everything is available in our nursery.*

> *I have the confidence to work with the children without waiting for the experts, and now have strategies to try. If they don't work, I can try something else.*

> *I see the importance of observation as the starting point for planning the next step for a child.*

> *There are simple things I can do which will make a difference.*

These course participants had just spent time seeing how language can be developed in PE and parachute sessions, with the magnetic board and through tabletop activities. No special equipment or additional expense was called for. The style of mediation was the key difference.

Jill's commentary:
1 Hayley is playing alone quite happily, unaware of Jill sitting nearby watching and wanting to interact and intervene in play.
2 Jill moves closer to see what she is playing with and join her (still on own agenda). She is moving animals without clear focus or play intention/sequences.

3 Jill picks up the large elephant and says 'Look, my elephant is eating – yum yum.' Hayley looks at the elephant eating and smiles.

4 Jill says 'Oh no! My elephant has eaten all the food!', using voice, facial expressions to emphasise laughing. At last eye contact, social smiles and responses! She is relaxed, unpressurised and happy to respond to join in fun. Beginning of play interaction and useful language exchange.

Socialising solo activity

The session with cognitive materials might go something like this. Usually nursery staff agree that the cognitive materials like jigsaws and sorting and matching tasks are often left out for children to tackle and enjoy by themselves. Frequently such self-correcting materials are the favourites for children with communication difficulties; they can enjoy the sense of success without the stress of talking. So often, the quieter the child, the more questions s/he gets. Faced with little response, adults tend to talk to fill the gaps and avoid awkward silences. Lopsided conversations then occur. Mutual discomfort can then lead to embarrassed withdrawal on both sides.

Normally, adult intervention might demonstrate good handling or arranging of pieces and aim to mediate strategies for successful completion. By contrast, our sugges-tion is to look at the activity as a chance to encourage turn-taking and conversation rather than simply to secure cognitive skill or the successful completion of a task. Once the participants look at it in this way, they generate many ideas on socialising solo activity.

For example, start with a complete puzzle and in turn claim a piece, the adult framing the script, e.g. 'I choose . . .'; then replace the pieces in turn, jointly celebrating the com-pletion of the work. Not all the pieces need be taken out – perhaps just the rim or the top line or one image or the red bits. Gradually without formal prompting, the child starts echoing key words, phrases and even sentences, e.g. 'my turn, red one, a top piece, I choose the red ball'. With beads, have a string each and take turns to choose a colour and follow the leader, rejoicing in the 'sameness' of our parallel strings. Resist the urge to correct and question and teach! Just model and comment on turns and choices. Resist the urge to overload the conversation. Only talk when it is your turn to choose; be quiet while the two of you watch closely. Keep to the 'watch then do' pattern. Remember it is hard to watch, listen, respond, and think of a reply, all at once – especially if there is little time to keep up. Take time.

Interest boxes and story bags

These boxes are used for highlighting concepts, verbs and vocabulary while practising listening, attention and turn-taking skills. We have colour boxes and texture boxes; we have collections of rhyming objects (e.g. bell/shell) and those with the same initial sound; we group objects with their verbs and with their functions. So, soap, hairbrush, tissue, cup, biscuit and book are linked with wash, brush, wipe, drink, eat, and read.

More care needs to be taken in mediating these concepts perhaps because it is harder to resist the 'teach and test' formula. If children are taking turns in a small group game to pick the appropriate object, there is the possibility of error to deal with. We tend to model the correct answer rather than highlight the choice as a mistake. Group sessions inevitably introduce waiting for your turn rather than taking rhythmical turns with one partner, and boredom can disrupt attention.

Of course, songs, games and stories come to our rescue. The magnetic board can illustrate the favourites by the display of visual prompts, pictures or symbols which the children can move about in unison with the words. We have found that the children in play time will gravitate to the board, unzip the magnetic pictures from their bags, enact the song and put the pieces away again at the end, all in the manner of the teacher. One child recently instructed two others to sit on their cushions while he ran through the sequence! Verbs are often learned in physical activities with the parachute and in music and movement. A daily dose of parachute play allows children to belong as they are joined in a circle. In this shared context, a wide range of language functions can find expression under the controlling guidance of the adult. Maintaining motivation through playfulness is our aim. Avoiding artificial communicating styles is the challenge we face. We are bound to come up against predicaments and choices.

Reflecting on 'critical incidents' (Tripp 1993) or 'professional predicaments' (Katz 1995)

Following an example set by Norwegian colleagues (Birkeland 2001), we used stories to aid our staff reflections. Stories of practice give a picture of relationships between children and their teachers and can be classified into various types. Birkeland, for example, is still generating types of story from her collection in kindergartens:

- sunny stories
- success stories
- turning-point stories
- blunder stories or
- routine stories.

The classification is neither complete nor exhaustive but certain stories are useful at different points in staff training. Different stories call for different responses. Some ask for confirmation and celebration. Others need confrontation and contrast (Bruner 1996) in order to start reflection. Routine stories, which rehearse the same impressions of children, need opening up to new perspectives. If sunny stories predominate, it could mean there is a lack of consciousness of problems rather than that all is well. The art of using such stories is in judging the mood of the professionals: is there a need for celebration to build confidence or challenge to find new ways? Reflective discussion needs to take place in a supportive ethos. Blunder stories need to be received without blame, and turning points need to flourish in a supportive climate. If the telling of failures reinforces a sense of incompetence, then no empowerment of staff can take place. It has been suggested that telling of dilemmas in anecdotes of practice allows *closeness* to the particularity and relevance of actual events as well as providing an *objective distance* (Eriksen 2001). Once in story form, everyone can concentrate on giving her point of view, and different interpretations can emerge, producing the necessary contrasts and facets. It helps to dispel the notion of a right and wrong way of doing things. Possibilities for change arise rather than unhelpful prescriptions or reprimands. Shared ownership of problems is more reassuring than shouldering burdens alone (see Hanko 1999).

Reflective questions move away from probes into an individual's motivations and mistakes; they try instead to prompt general discussion about practice around the instance.

The sort of questions might include:

- What questions does this story prompt?
- What understandings does it bring?
- What is pleasing (worrying, baffling) about this story?
- What do you think the other characters in the story would say?
- How might they tell a different story?
- How could it have a different beginning or ending?
- Are any changes in our way of working suggested by the story?

Such questions illuminate complexities and mutual influences within a system. What happens in one part of a system can have an impact on another, and no one person is responsible or culpable alone.

There follow some examples of stories that prompted reflection on our practice.

The story of the toothbrush and the broom: grasping the concept of big and little

The points made by the four of us are amalgamated in the account below. There are many instances of our children failing to appreciate this relative concept in spite of games around our concept box. Ideally, we would use (and suggest parents use) life experiences as they happen, before you 'manufacture' them, e.g. using a *big* towel and a *little* one at bath time. Such concepts are best absorbed in relation to the child's whole body, e.g., take a *big* step or a *little* one.

Once in class, however, constraints of time and space reduce such opportunities for child-centred learning. Although it is known that ' you start with the child for effective learning', the well-meaning teacher can 'grasp control', in an attempt 'to teach or draw out knowledge'.

While recognising that a toy cow is much smaller than the real thing, we would always contrast a big with a small replica of the animal. It is always presented in a comparative frame and is determined by what is available in the classroom. When the children fail, is it because they have not had the pragmatic experience early on? Is it a stage missed or did they have the experience but missed the significance; are they still missing the significance? Is it a matter of not being 'ready to perceive' the significance? Are we 'flogging a dead horse' by pushing the concept when it is clearly not being absorbed? Because it is an area shown to be lacking, do we feel 'we *should* be teaching it' and emphasise the teaching of it. When we pass on to teachers a proposed individual plan, it is easier to pass on the target in terms of concepts to be gained with suitable activities than to guess at the pragmatic possibilities available in their contexts. We do not know the skills and personal qualities of the staff implementing suggestions. It is difficult therefore to make written plans which are 'transferable and manageable'.

So this instance prompted much wondering about the teaching of concepts.

The story of spinning

The video clip of a boy endlessly spinning the roundabout has prompted much reflection. He is seen commandeering the toy and resisting the intervener's suggestions to give the toy-people a spin or to co-opt another child to take turns in the activity. He becomes even more determined to take the wheel to a safe place to spin it without interruption. Suggestions from conference members opened up some new possibilities. What if we were to 'join' the child and show an emotional interest in his fascination, making comments like, 'Wow! How fast it goes!' Others wondered about using his emerging skill with scissors to create a paper windmill that would spin as you blew. Taking turns to blow and spin the wheel might socialise this interest. Another suggestion was to make colour-matching lotto more motivating by having a spinning dice. Because he is seen elsewhere on the video managing to colour-match the balloons and to throw the dice in turn, it would be possible to build on his strengths and legitimise spinning in this social context. What had been seen as an unhelpful obsession to be curtailed, new eyes saw as a fascination that could motivate learning.

We considered approaches to absorbing rituals. We have pieces of equipment which allow 'social experience *plus* spinning'. We have used cogs; the helter-skelter marble run, snakes cut out in spirals that twirl in the air. As children progress to games with rules, there are twisters and spinning dice. In this case, however, we knew that parental wish was to ban spinning so this behaviour had already become a contentious area. Parents do want to see unacceptable behaviours controlled so this makes for hard decisions.

We agreed that we did not want to do anything that would make an obsession more obsessional, but that we aimed to make such behaviours less solitary and more social. Our daily practice of introducing the order of events in a time line of symbols, and ensuring an initial choice of activity from an array of picture choices on offer has helped by giving an alternative structure and an expectation of change. Tactfully a child who has played exclusively in the water is lured to the neighbouring finger painting table, first to watch his favourite letter drawn, then to put his hand on top of the helping adult's hand and finally to risk touching the paint – a new and frightening experience! A loud 'no' became a tentative 'yes'.

We began to think of the emotional function of ritualistic and repetitive behaviours. Hand-flapping could be an undesirable behaviour to suppress or it could be a signal of anxiety or pleasure. Were these behaviours personal rituals for comfort in predictability or was there an element of attention-seeking and deliberate provocation? We were more hopeful about changing an attention-seeking ploy than a conditioned and comforting habit (for attention-seeking, see Mellor 1997).

We used to adopt the view that we could 'allow the fascination', but only as a 'reward for conformity, after achievement of our set task'. Perhaps we are now (along with other professionals) beginning to analyse the function of such behaviours. 'As our skills, expertise and knowledge develop alongside other professionals', we are starting to see such behaviours as *a trigger or a cause or a communication* which needs considering' (Jill).

For example, was the boy who sang the wrong song at the wrong time (and wrecked singing time by his distress when stopped) indicating a need to keep control? Could this need have been met if we had allowed him to sit in the teacher's chair and *lead* the singing? The other children were then likely to follow him happily, for the exact order was of no consequence to them. This was a radical suggestion, which could be dismissed as impractical or be heralded as a creative opportunity out of a negative stalemate.

The boy who had a 'last night I had a dream' obsession was very quickly drawn out of it when he was humorously joined with a competing story on the same pattern. Soon, he was able to say, 'Jill, we are not talking about that!' The table had been turned and some insight about the effect of talking without listening gained. Here was a success story to reflect on. This child could cope with humour; telling his type of stories took away his solitary platform for commanding adult attention. He was learning to take turns rather than physically pulling adults' faces to 'listen to me!'

All these complex reflections were prompted by differing responses to the same story. The chance to be reflective was welcomed but there was a feeling that it was a pity that we had dwelt on our shortcomings when we have so many successes to celebrate. This unease suggests that the balance of stories was not quite right on this occasion. Some more success stories were needed to bolster 'the secure self' which can be 'open to experience, daring to risk' (Holly 1989: 74).

The fact that busy professionals gave up their lunch-time to discuss these predicaments indicates a 'commitment to systematic, self-critical enquiry, founded in curiosity and the wish to understand' (ibid.: 71).

When 'the mind focuses on setting problems and enquiring into possible solutions: the teacher theorises' (ibid.: 73).

Here, the gap between theory and practice closes, and considered professional action can proceed directly.

Telling others the timetable: 'It's juice time.'

He has come out of himself. He would never have stood in front of a group and done the finger puppets. He is singing and talking all the time, without having to press him. (Parent)

The adult plays in the sand, making her dragonfly land on someone's head.

He has realised the power of language and that he can effect change. This also means, of course, that he can use words to refuse! He tries out ways of saying things and corrects himself. He has loved coming, running in without clinging. He is now speaking out in his group at nursery. There have always been things he could do at nursery and he would willingly show his work, but he did not know what to do with the praise; he would clam up. (Parent)

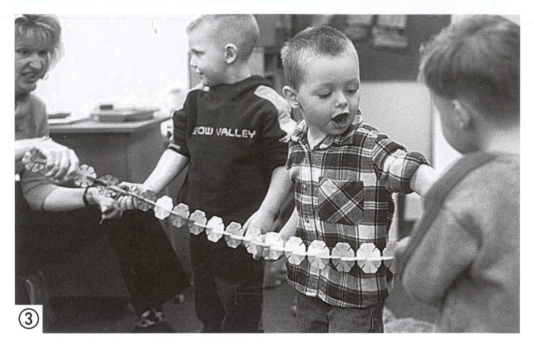

The group dynamic/suspense: how long before our chain will break?

His responses are completely changed. He used to ignore our questions, and not take any notice of you. He would play on his own and not want help. Everyone at school and relatives who have not seen him for a while have commented on the change in him. He even says things like, 'excuse me'! (Parent)

Each of the eight children has a turn. The others practise good sitting and good listening from their individual cushions in a circle.

2: Between Clinic and Classroom

This section derives from conversing with Di Nicholson about working across the disciplines in language units in mainstream schools. As a teacher/speech and language therapist, she already has fused two perspectives. She knows how it feels to be in both roles and therefore promotes sensitive, interprofessional working. This is a gap she has closed in her own dealings. She takes up the story in her own voice:

The therapist or support teacher is presented with a unique opportunity to engage very small groups of children in more detailed, elaborate and enviable activities than would normally be possible within a large classroom. They are also in a good position to make use of games (whether oral, on boards or through card games) than most class teachers. This ability to produce enviable pieces of work while at the same time systematically tackling the heart of a child's difficulties is seen by most class teachers to be of great value, and since they recognise the format, they are hopefully reassured that their children are getting the right type of input. This means that teachers are more likely to become supportive and enthusiastic about the work of therapists (and support teachers), and the important partnership between teacher and therapist can really take off. In the best instances it is not long before the teacher can spontaneously begin to spot opportunities, however small, for the integration of the work into the child's school day. This, of course, is music to the therapist's ear, since one of the biggest problems is how to fit the therapy aims into an overloaded school day without the teacher having a nervous breakdown! It is vital to be led by teachers as to what is feasible for them, and it will necessarily differ from teacher to teacher.

> *One teacher I know had the most amazing ability to translate my aims into astonishing games in her reception class. I once gave her a couple of standard ideas for a child one week, and when I returned she had rigged up an electrical matching game in which lights lit up if the child made the right responses in a phonological task. 'Well, it fitted into the science', she explained.*

Children who come back into class with something different and interesting in hand usually attract a crowd of envious others demanding to know when they will be getting the opportunity. This makes sure that the child in question is seen as getting special and important time. They become elevated in the eyes of the rest of the class and the subject of awe and envy. This has to be good for feelings of self-worth.

> *I worked with a boy who found just about everything hard at school. He had got to the point where he was quite challenging in class and his self-esteem was plummeting. My nursery nurse who was doing some one to one with him decided that they would do a new and exciting project. Together they made a huge papier-mâché Frankenstein which had all the boy's troublesome sound targets incorporated within it in some way. The interesting thing for me was the look of relief on his face at being taken out when she came to get him, and the look of total pride as his friends examined the progress of his work on his return.*

If I can, I get a bit of display area in the classroom which the targeted child or children can build up with their work. The other class members usually want to be involved giving a perfect opportunity to boost the status of the target child/children by allowing them to decide if other children can contribute.

For busy therapists with only limited time with children, there is often a feeling of urgency to use the opportunity to maximise the times that a child gets to rehearse a target in the particular session. The danger in this is that the interest of the child can take a back seat in favour of activities which are seen to provide for this. There can be an over-reliance, for instance, on the use of line drawings or boxes of cards which may provide maximum opportunities for drilling, but are soon both boring and unrelated to the child's interests or understanding of the world.

I am sometimes asked how I fit in making things with children (particularly things which include painting.) I explain that it is not simply a case of fitting it in, but more of a case of it being essential that children are given the types of task which they recognise and can interact with. Similarly it is essential that therapist and child have something to talk about. I prioritise this need for a shared communicative intent over the number of times a child has had opportunity to hit his or her target in a session.

Di was sure that her subsequent training as a teacher had 'revolutionised' her approach to working with children with speech and language difficulties. She feels that she learned about motivation and differentiation and group management from teacher training and this has enabled her to enjoy group project work and see its benefits. Before she had dual training, she envied the teacher's position, because children confided more in their teachers and developed better conversations in the course of their shared activities.

Having a project structure to her therapy time (with continuity from week to week) has allowed her to enter into a working relationship with a group of children. She aims to give 'something of herself' to each child and not be afraid to discuss personal feelings and her own mistakes. She gives feedback to children about their strengths and weaknesses in this spirit of joint reflection. She finds that if she has had dialogues with children about matters of shared importance, then 'the rules of relationships kick in' like not letting your friends down and respecting them. This means that children then accept the discipline, because they know you can also be friendly and caring. In the frame of a relationship, she finds it hard to sit a child in front of her and give him task after task to complete as in a formal assessment. She owns that this is probably a 'reflection on my personality as much as anything'.

So, she has insisted that her 'therapy' room be arranged like a classroom with display boards, designated work areas, cupboards full of consumables like paint, glue, felt tips, scissors, clay, tissue paper, crayons, etc. She introduces the children to the room, showing them where to hang up coats, where to sit and explains the rules and expectations needed for sharing space to engage in an art/craft activity together.

Time is carefully managed and children learn the 'shape of the sessions'. She 'hooks them into understanding a context' before thinking about what words or sounds are to be learned. The timetable and routines do not vary and each session has an explicit beginning, middle and end, with a 'plan, do, review' structure. The familiar room and recognisable 'friends' and predictable sequence of events around a purposeful activity reassure children with language comprehension difficulties.

Each child knows his/her own special targets in terms of words to know or sounds to practice. Everyone is on the alert to participate as the occasion demands. Everyone is also aware of the others' special aims and is at the ready to help and prompt. Because the focus is on a common activity, the group 'sees the point' of being together. The joint task in hand unites and galvanises the group and there is the expectation that everyone will make the effort to speak and participate. For example, if the 's' sound is your practice sound, to use the *s*taples or *s*ellotape you must try the sound to secure the item you need. Making masks together would mean much incidental use of the 'f' sound as *f*eathers and *f*ox entered the scene.

She cautions against believing that groups are always motivating in this way:

> *There are two sorts of groups: the demotivating and the motivating ones. The demotivating ones are the ones where it is not planned, where it is not differentiated appropriately, where it is not thought through and where children do an awful lot of waiting their turn to have a go. If you have a game which involves picking a card and saying the word and if you have six kids, at any given point, five of them aren't doing anything; then it is utterly boring and there is no structure to it . . .*

Individual planning happens prior to the start of the intervention, and suitable targets and materials are ready to hand. Within these set parameters, there is room for the sudden flash of inspiration in response to a spontaneous happening. It is not opportunist or *laissez-faire* but carefully designed. Behind the apparently lucky chance for incidental learning, is a tight structure and exact preparation.

Thus, the context is both a physical environment and a social one. The cohesive theme evolves over six–eight weeks in hourly sessions. Children arrive keyed up to continue the project which could be around a shared book, with extension activities involving drama, model-making, music and painting. The common task is 'real', not 'a false scenario'. It is designed 'to prompt talking' and 'give ongoing opportunities to talk'. Working like this has got around the problem which bedevils much of traditional speech and language therapy delivery: 'transfer of skills from the clinic to the outside world'. It was 'brilliant' to see the children walking out of the therapy classroom wearing their masks and

> *[to] hear them talking to their parents with the correct words all the way down the corridor, out and about, and they took the masks to school and then they had to describe them in front of the class, remembering the words.*

She knows that the children are able to do this because they have learned within a communicative context, which has a 'sequence to it, a form to it, a story to it' and they see the 'point' of it. This is very different from teaching isolated skills, which do not have 'a real conversational social context and the children do it like parrots' without being engaged. With 'gentle promptings in the social scenario', the children get it right and then because it's very like the social scenario that they are walking out into, the generalisation is easier. There is a greater chance of their learning bridging the gap between the clinic and the classroom.

CHAPTER 6

Special Time: What's Special about Special Time

Tina Cook

The nursery is decked out for autumn. There have been lots of discussions about autumn colours, reds, browns and orange. Now the children have dispersed to their various activities. Sam is drawing with a large black pencil-crayon. He works intently giving the project his undivided attention. Another child is at the table. Occasionally the other child looks at Sam, but Sam does not look up. An adult comes to the table and has a conversation with the other child and then moves over to look at Sam's complex design of interlinked and overlapping lines.

'That's lovely Sam, but it's all in black and we have lots of other colours. Why don't you try using some other colours? The yellow or the orange? Here's the orange. Would you like to try that?'

Sam doesn't answer the adult. Sam doesn't look up. The adult, not getting a response, watches Sam for about 30 seconds, then goes to talk to another child.

Sam is 3½ years old and has not yet spoken or looked at anyone apart from his mother. When he speaks to his mother he stares deep into her eyes and gives one-word commands such as 'custard' or 'bed'. Sam has been referred to the 'Communication Group'. He will have some 'Special Time'.

Introduction

This is the story of how a group of people came to use 'Special Times' to work with children displaying behaviours that could indicate a specifically diagnosable communication disorder. The term Special Time has many meanings in general use, but in this instance it describes the use of a non-directive approach to play that provides children with an arena for beginning to understand communication (Cockerill n.d.).

This chapter describes how Cockerill originally envisaged the programme called 'Special Times' and how it has been adapted in use by early years professionals and practitioners working in the North East of England. Over time, the name has been slightly adapted and it has come to be known locally as 'Special Time'. This chapter documents how Special Time, used alongside other communicative environments, can help a child with severe communication/social difficulties to begin to recognise that within the intricacies of complex reciprocal information exchanges, there is a routine and a structure that they can understand. It highlights the opportunities offered by Special Time. It addresses learning and teaching issues that arise from working with children for whom communication has become a frustration and a barrier to accessing their environment and learning. It explores the relationship between the skills we as adults have and how we use those skills. In particular, it looks at how adults work together with children to develop functional communication links and the effect of culturally shaped social behaviour on that co-construction. Finally, it asks what is special about Special Time and how a programme that is deemed 'special' can be part of a pedagogical framework that develops understandings of inclusive practice.

Background

At the beginning of the 1990s I was working as head of a pre-school service for children with special educational needs in Newcastle upon Tyne. Prior to this, my experience as a 'special educator' was varied. I have worked with children aged from 17 years to birth, in that order. As I became more experienced in working with children, my interest in communication developed. I use the word 'communication' carefully, because my interest lies not only in the words children use, but how they use them and if they don't use words, how do children communicate in other ways? How do children crack an adult-centred, culturally biased communication code? How can we help them to understand and use communicative interactions if they find the code confusing and alienating?

Communication is complex. It involves joint attention, joint interest and a willingness to share understandings; it involves watching, listening and waiting; it involves initiation and reciprocation; it involves making meaning of abstract signals and it might involve talking. Talking that does not *engage* at least two people is not communication.

At the beginning of the 1990s, the pre-school service had been increasingly concerned about the number of very young children referred to us who were having difficulties with understanding the two-way nature of communication. Many of the children referred to us were, at the age of three, already intensely frustrated, anxious, angry and withdrawn. We began to think about ways we could work with and understand more about the needs of these children and how we could provide for them more effectively. This concern was shared by other services in the city that came into contact with young children and their families, specifically the speech and language therapy service and the educational psychologists. Limited in what we could do alone, the three services came together to pool their expertise and resources to support children with severe communication/social difficulties and their families.

It was at this point that the speech and language therapist with whom we were working introduced us to non-directive play therapy or 'Special Time'. Special Time was to become a central tenet of the group work the three services were to offer children and families.

Special Time

When working as head of the Communication Therapy Department at the Cheyne Centre in London, Helen Cockerill developed her ideas, alongside those of co-workers in the centre, about how to work with children with speech and language difficulties in a non-directive manner. She called this way of working 'Special Times'. Special Times aim:

> [to] encourage initiation: to help the child realise s/he can be an effective communicator . . . to help the child understand the power of communication. Special Times also have a positive effect on a child's functioning in areas such as play, interaction and nonverbal communication, in addition to linguistic skills. (Cockerill n.d.: 2)

The Special Time programme can look deceptively simple. A child is in a room with a selection of toys and an adult commentates on their behaviour/play. The adult does not give instruction or try to direct play in any way, but comments on what the child does in 'an interested manner'. This lasts for about 40 minutes. Special Time is, however, a highly skilled and demanding practice, as anyone who has been using it will tell you. It has been used in mainstream and special schools, nurseries, playgroups and with individuals. Generally practitioners begin somewhat doubtfully but often return with stories of success with a wide variety of children. We have used the approach with children with different forms of communication difficulties, including a child with Down's Syndrome who was a good communicator but did not use language. Giving her the opportunity to hear the same word/s over and over again at her instigation and at her pace was a fun game for her. It very quickly resulted in her saying the word/s to herself as she played before eventually going on to initiate a communication using words as requests.

Special Time: the group programme

Each term, six pre-school children with identified social/communication needs and their families were invited by the three services to attend six group sessions. Each session was 1½ hours long, the first 40 minutes being Special Time. Representatives from each child's playgroup/nursery and other services working with the child were invited to attend one of the six sessions. The number of sessions provided was a purely pragmatic response determined by the time the three services felt they could offer, the size of the room and the number of children on the waiting list. We used a group approach with the children because Helen Cockerill's original suggestion of individual work with children was beyond our resources. Given the profiles of the children referred to the group, we optimistically called it the 'Communication Group' and then were surprised many times by the aptness of this title. We discovered that the group environment did enable this set of children to begin to socialise and communicate with their peers. This was something that, with this set of children, we had mistakenly suspected would not be possible at this stage of their communicative development.

Special Time should preferably always take place at the same time, in the same room and with the same people, to remove any ambiguity for the children about what is going to take place. While our group always met in the same room, there were often different adults in the room. Volunteers were invited in order to have sufficient adults to commentate on the children. These were often speech and language therapy students, keen to extend their own experience, but adults from the children's nurseries and playgroups sometimes participated too. All parents were invited to be in with the children at least once during the programme. This variation in adults seemed to make very little difference to the children unless the adult was their own parent in which case some children would gravitate towards them. The children were also unconcerned about the half-term break that usually fell during the run of six sessions. It would appear that the constancy of the environment itself was sufficiently supportive to enable the children to continue with the routine of the morning.

Ways of signalling the beginning and end of Special Time are important to identify and separate it from general play time. In our case, Special Time was only 40 minutes of a 1½-hour programme. To ensure that the children knew when it was coming to an end they were first informed verbally that the session was nearly over, then the room was cleared of the particular set of toys used for Special Time. The routine of 'finish' was maintained despite protests when a favourite toy was taken away. The disappearance of the toys, followed by the introduction of juice and snack where the children were directed to sit and participate, were clear signs of the change in programme.

When, later on, we wanted to use this approach in a child's pre-school setting, a clear physical marker such as a mat rolled out at a certain time, or a specific box of toys only used for 'Special Time', helped the children understand the nature of the session and clearly signalled the start and finish.

During Special Time the children are free to do whatever they like within the environment as long as it is not dangerous. They choose an activity, or not, as the case may be. Some do very little to begin with, and this is accepted. Following much discussion we decided to allow children to engage in self-stimulating behaviours such as flapping and jumping, as long as they were not hurting either themselves or others. The sessions are about developing communicative understandings. Their focus is not behaviour management or cognitive development, although ultimately they have a significant effect on both. As the children amuse themselves, an adult provides a running commentary to each child on the activity they have chosen, whether that is running up and down, jumping on the spot, playing with the Duplo farm, etc. The ground rules for the running commentary are: the adult must be totally focused on producing the words for the child that correlate to that child's current interest, behaviour and play; it can include signing if that is considered appropriate; the adult must not ask a child questions about their play, make any suggestions about the play or interpret for a child what they might want to do with the toys and they must not direct a child's attention to anything in particular. The adult's role is to be non-invasive, non-intrusive, but practical and flexible, to take language back to its core, so that it can have meaning and hence become a communication. It is exhausting and can be physically quite hard work, especially with very active children. The sheer intensity of concentrating on another person to determine their interest and find words to describe their activity is draining.

Special Time: the role of families and practitioners

Families generally began by observing Special Time from behind a one-way mirror. Members of staff (an educational psychologist and a teacher) spent time with families and the invited practitioners from the child's daily setting as they watched the children together. For most families, and indeed practitioners, it was the first time they had seen their children without the children being aware of their presence. Some were surprised at how well their children continued without them, others were saddened when they saw how little their child interacted with others. This time offered an opportunity to talk both with professionals and with other parents, about their children's communication and associated behaviours. The adults discussed what they saw, what that might mean for the child and for their own behaviour when with the child and how they felt about the non-directive process.

A casual observer can underrate the vital role adults play in Special Time. Comments have been made suggesting that the adult 'does very little'. In fact, the adult's work is the crux of the programme. It is not working towards catching the observable, planned, active work that is often used as a measure of input in more formal assessments, but how an adult responds in a situation, often in a very subtle way, that indicates the quality of the work.

Following the third group session parents were invited to participate in the non-directive session. Most parents found this difficult. They wanted to try and engage with their child, to help them play and communicate in a way they saw as appropriate. The non-directive adult behaviour was alien to the way they would choose to be with their child. Many found it embarrassing and some were put off by knowing that a number of people were watching them through the mirror.

We all, practitioners and family members alike, found it very hard to avoid directing the children, asking them questions or making 'interested' suggestions. Adults seem to be programmed to direct children. We want to help children develop their play and communication and do this by offering ideas and suggestions to try and pull the child into a social situation. In their work using intensive interaction, Nind and Hewitt (1996) struggled with achieving a similar form of non-directiveness which they called 'task-lessness'. They suggest that our previous experiences and our training have turned us into 'people who dominate and control the learning' (1996: 186). We believe it is our 'job' to set and direct tasks.

We also appear to be programmed to ask questions: that's a big teddy, isn't it?, What's that you've made?, Would you like to play with this?, Why don't we make the farmer go on the tractor?, Can you find the last piece of jigsaw?, Would you stop flapping your hands now? According to Cockerill (n.d.: 6), 'The ability to remain totally non-directive may require a lot of practice, but it's fundamental to the technique. It is what makes Special Times different to other interactions.'

As Special Time progressed, the adults increasingly recognised the importance of trying to ascertain what might be interesting a child about a certain activity. This enabled them to be more sensitive in giving a child the word for the action/object that interests the child rather than offering what an adult might see as interesting. After beginning to use Special Time principles in her playgroup, one worker noted that she now felt more comfortable being with a particular child.

> *The idea of a running commentary has made me more communicative and relaxed with Steven. Before I didn't know what to do with him so I just didn't say anything if I was near him. Now I do a running commentary and I am more relaxed – it's bringing us together.*

When children have insufficient communication skills to initiate and develop effective communication themselves, adults tend to have two main responses to this. One is to become more directive in the process of engineering communication, especially verbal communication, and to bombard a child with ideas and questions. The second is to withdraw from the situation because you are not getting feedback from a child. In these circumstances the adult becomes confused and may even feel rejected by the child. Both responses have a significant effect on the communicative environment offered to children, reducing opportunities to engage in relaxed communicative situations that the child might begin to understand and make meaning of.

One parent recognised that not only had he fallen into not conversing very much with his only child but also that, as a household, they were not very verbal. His response to his observation on their communicative behaviour as a family group was to begin to commentate on his own actions as well as those of his children. The first example he gave was of reading the paper:

> *[N]ow when I pick up the paper I don't just do it, I say, 'Daddy's sitting down' or 'Daddy's picking up the paper', 'Daddy's reading the paper' – and John looks at me when I say that. Before he wouldn't bother to look at me at all.*

During the Special Time programme, parents, nursery and playgroup staff were all encouraged to use the principles of Special Time within their own setting. It surprised us all how sometimes a very small change in adult behaviour, a change that generally involved trying to find a child's wavelength and behave accordingly, led to massive strides being made by the child in beginning to understand the adult and indeed other children. Practitioners have also reported how, through reflecting on their own skills and knowledge of the development of communication, and applying it more rigorously within the nursery/playgroup, other children they work with have benefited in immediate and observable ways.

Special Time: a special pedagogy?

I have been describing a group process that has taken place outside 'mainstream' settings. While all the children were in a mainstream playgroup or nursery, the practice of Special Time temporarily removed them from that environment. In asking myself critical questions about this work and whether it was further stigmatising and isolating this group of children, I began by reflecting critically on the pedagogical aspect of the process and how it might relate to early years practice. Here pedagogy is defined as 'Any conscious activity by one person designed to enhance the learning of another'

(Mortimore 1999: 17). In their work, Lewis and Norwich (1999) found that while there is a lack of evidence to support special educational needs specific pedagogies there is 'a persistent sense that special education means special pedagogy to many teachers and researchers' (1999: 3).

In looking at the pedagogy of Special Time as we had developed it, I wanted to know if anything was truly 'special' or 'different' from the everyday work and interaction of adults with children. In the following sections I look at the main component parts of Special Time and consider the interplay between the knowledge adults have of communication development and when and how they are likely to use that knowledge.

Linking words to actions

One of the aims of Special Time is to help children recognise a link between words and objects or actions by association. Through paring down everyday language and only offering the child access to critical information-carrying words it aims to enable a child to develop the understanding that a particular word stands for a particular object or action. For instance, when a child is putting the plug in the play sink the words 'plug in' are heard and when they take it out, they hear 'plug out'. If the name of an action is repeated when the child initiates that action, the link between word and action is immediate and direct. Initially only one word is used to reduce confusion. 'Walking' rather than 'you're walking' or 'sitting' rather than 'sitting down'. Extra flourishes are removed. Gradually the commentator may add more complex utterances as the child begins to make more meaning from the language.

For most children, learning that words stand for objects takes place when they are very young. The Special Time programme presumes that this has not taken place effectively and a functional link has not been made. It is not uncommon for children with autistic spectrum disorders to have language but the language they use may have no meaning for them. They are empty words: strings of words they have heard and utilise. Sometimes their use of words can seem appropriate. For example, one young boy, when noticing it was raining, always said: 'It's raining, when it rains my grandmother uses her umbrella.' A slightly odd phrase for a three and a half-year-old, but not out of context. When used every time it rains with no other sentence being substituted for it, it becomes very unusual. By breaking the sentence down it was clear that the boy had no understanding of the meaning of 'raining' or 'uses', but he did know that this was what you said when the water came out of the sky.

This method mimics the role of parents with young children. As young children play among a pile of toys, parents commentate on what they are playing with. They also commentate on children's activities: 'whoops a daisy – fallen down', 'you're giving me your cup – thank you', 'what a lovely smile'. As the children play, they start to show the adult what they are playing with, and the adult naturally comments on that with 'book', 'Bob the Builder' or whatever happens to be in fashion at the time. Children often 'show' with their food and it is no surprise that biscuit, cup and apple are some children's first words. Nor is it a surprise that the naming word for close relatives is high up on the list of first words because, apart from the phonological simplicity of words such as 'dadda', these words tend to be used repetitively by adults in the presence of children. Unfortunately, this also is the case with words like 'no' so perhaps we have something to learn here!

Learning within your comfort zone

Special Time offers an environment where children are not asked to communicate beyond their abilities, beyond where they are comfortable. They are not questioned before they understand either the words in the questioning sentence, or the concept of a question. When talking to young babies, while we ask them endless questions, we do not expect an answer (generally we answer our own questions when talking with young babies). By streamlining our language and emphasising the key information-carrying words we regulate our language to enable babies both to understand and learn. We are unlikely to use complex conversational constructions with the very young (or indeed adults who do not understand our language). In the Special Time environment we are trying to emulate the streamlined nature and directness of such speech, to regulate our language and not offer children complex linguistic strings that confuse and frustrate meaning-making.

Repetition

During Special Time the same words may be repeated hundreds of times. Again, this emulates what we do with young children. If we think of the activities young babies are engaged in, they are very repetitive. The things we do with young children are equally repetitive, nursery rhymes and books such as *We're Going on a Bear Hunt* (Rosen 1993). Young children may do the same things over and over again (Athey 1990; Nutbrown 1994) and love to hear the same book over and over again. It is part of the learning process.

Consistency

Special Time should preferably take place in the same environment with as few changes as possible. If we change an environment and its components regularly, children have to expend energy working out where they are and what is expected of them. Keeping the environment the same enables the child to focus on other aspects of the experience. If changes need to be made, for instance, a room or personnel change, the consistence of the toys can be that bridge. Again, if we think of young babies, their early life often consists of many routines. If we are going somewhere new we try and minimise uncertainty for them by taking familiar toys/blankets, etc. If they have to stay out overnight, we might take their own cot rather than use a substitute or we might prepare them for the change by putting them to sleep in the travel cot in their own room for a few days before we take the travel cot somewhere else.

By thinking about what makes children feel secure we can use this in our work with children who, because they cannot necessarily understand what is happening around them by piecing together visual and verbal clues, have high levels of insecurity (Frith 1990). Using routine and visual cues and clues is one of the main principles behind The Treatment and Education of Autistic and related Communication Handicapped Children (TEACCH) programme. Most people need some order in their lives. Many children (and adults) benefit from an ordered situation although we must be careful not to hem children into boundaries created by predetermined adult preoccupations. We need to leave space for creative and imaginative thinking.

Learning best from what you are interested in

Young children are self-motivated to learn (Gopnik *et al.* 1999) and we know that children learn best when they are interested in the activity (Fisher 1996; Reggio Children 1997). Children, particularly those with autistic spectrum disorders, often have unexpected foci of interest or difficulties in locating an 'interesting' feature: 'When somebody points something out to me that I find interesting, I always have trouble finding it. It's especially when I think it might be interesting. I could see something boring straight away' (narrator in Arnall and Webb 1992). Special Time tries to offer an environment where children can demonstrate their interests and as a result, perhaps by default, they directly manipulate the language they hear. When babies/young children cry to be fed, they are then fed, and the words around them are about hunger, food and drink. The words are about the thing they have initiated. If we watch babies we see that while there are some things that parents have to do, and so get done despite the baby (shopping, cooking, changing nappies, etc.), the baby is a very strong manipulator of its environment. In so doing babies are also manipulating the communication towards things they are interested in.

Language and communication as a co-constructed exchange

For communication to take place, language has to be part of an interchange, a social interchange that involves both parties. In the early 1990s I made my first visit to a *casa d' copii* (House of the Children) in Alexandria, Romania. This particular *casa* is for children from birth to four years old. At this time the babies 0–9 months old spent both days and nights in their cots, often two or even three to a cot. The older children, when not in their cots, were confined to rooms bare of toys or even furniture. The children tended to sit quietly, rocking and staring or they might behave in aggressive ways towards other children and adults, particularly new adults. The role of the adults who worked with the children was complex. They had to feed, clothe, wash and organise groups of up to 25 children. Their shifts were long, often 12 hours without a break. While they told the children what to do, 'come and get washed', 'sit on your potty', and they talked among themselves, sitting down, cuddling and communicating with a child were not part of the daily routine. All but a handful of children were unable to initiate, engage in, maintain or understand the to and fro of a communicative exchange.

In the next months and years, as circumstances changed and the adults began to engage with the children, talking to them and with them, singing songs and chanting traditional rhymes, the *casa d' copii* came alive once more with children eager to communicate with each other and the adults. For me this seemed a stark example of the importance of engagement in a communicative interchange. Words alone do not make for communication.

Most children attending the group had difficulties with understanding non-verbal communication exchanges. For many children eye contact, facial expression and general body language, the socially constructed clues for understanding messages without understanding language, complicated rather than supported meaning making. For others, socialisation had been affected by their inability to make sense of verbal communication. We witnessed children for whom other humans appeared to pose a threat. Some of the children had become intensely withdrawn with aggressive outbursts if their world was disturbed. Many children ignored other children and adults and intently and purposely went about their own business of play. How could we co-construct language with children for whom interaction with others had become something to be avoided?

Sometimes it may look as if Special Time divorces socialisation and communication from language. The practice appears to concentrate predominantly on an adult giving the child a word without any expectation of an interaction. When addressing the communication needs of the children, we discovered that socially recognised signs such as smiles, touch and tone were not necessarily going to support communication and were, in many cases, adding to the confusion. We therefore tried to start at a point where the children would feel comfortable in the co-construction of a communication, at a point where they were at ease with the social interaction, however distant that may seem to the adult. We were not denying the necessity of social interaction for communication but were engaging with the children at the level of social interaction with which they were comfortable. To co-construct a communication both parties need some influence over the composition of that construction. Special Time aims to use some of the known preferences of a child, the preference for repetition and routine, the preference not to engage in eye contact, the preference for a particular play regime, to begin to engage with the child. Our role as adults was to try and understand some of the complexities of the children's ways of being to enable a mutual interaction to take place. As one parent who attended the group said:

> *It took a long time before I realised it was me making him do all the hard work. Me the adult, was making him the 3½ year old, do all the work. He had to learn what I wanted him to learn, and because he found it hard, I made him do more of it. No wonder every time I started making him play with me, or even look at me, he just tried to run off. I would've in his situation.*

Special Time as a special curriculum

A central and challenging organisational principle of the Special Time curriculum is that the children should have control of their own play. The adult organises the environment and their own pedagogical behaviours, e.g. running commentary, to act as a framework of support, but the practice is open to the child's interpretation. This principle is inherent in other named practices. High Scope in particular uses the concept of children planning their own day around a given environment (Hohmann 1979). The children use the given framework in their own way with the adult tuning in to the child's interests and activity. One view of the curriculum (Rodger 1994: 15) is that it should encompass what the children know, do and understand in a range of learning areas. This offers a broad view of a curriculum that encompasses all opportunities and systems whose aim is to encourage learning.

We see that children are competent instigators of their own learning. We only need to watch a young baby design its own play for evidence of this (Gopnik *et al.* 1999: 86–7). We know that the stages of development as outlined by Piaget (1954) are not set in stone as 'must go through/if you haven't done this your development is arrested here forever' stages. While we do not have a template – a list of things you can do with a child that if you follow it, in that order, will ensure they reach a particular milestone – we may be able to develop a set of principles.

My own principles of practice are constantly being clarified and re-clarified but include:

1 Children are powerful instigators of their own learning and development.
2 The adult role is to observe and facilitate, sometimes to lead but not to dominate.
3 Adults must learn from children as children learn from adults.
4 Adults must think carefully about what they learn from children and what they do with that knowledge.

Where the curriculum starts and who has control of the curriculum then become embedded in a set of principles with the aim of developing understanding and meaning, rather than a set of outcomes.

What makes Special Time special?

I would argue that there are two important aspects of Special Time that make it special and both are to do with adult behaviours. The first is to do with how adults know what they know, and the second is to do with how they apply it. While working with a group of social service managers on an intensive interaction programme Nind and Hewitt (1996) recorded this intentionally ironic statement made by one of their course participants. This resonates with the experience of adults learning about Special Time: 'Well, we've finally done it. We've got people to come up here and train us in how to behave naturally' (ibid.: 3). Adults are generally exceptionally knowledgeable about how to support and facilitate children's communicative development. While the nature of communication is immeasurably complex, we all have strategies that we use to engage children (and adults) in a functional communicative interchange. We use them with infinite subtlety, sensitivity and perceptiveness. While not all communicative interactions are satisfactory, we can, and do, employ endless means of remedying unsuccessful interchanges. Such knowledge and skills need to be made explicit, to be interpreted and recognised as valuable ways of knowing that can be applied specifically and at will. Special Time helps us to pare down communicative situations to learn more about what we do instinctively as adults when we try to engage with other people.

The second aspect of what makes Special Time special is the application of knowledge. Our everyday communication is affected by socially constructed parameters. The social and cultural environment shapes our behaviours. While all cultures use speech as a communicator, there are many languages. Cultures also vary in the way they use body language and other non-verbal communication techniques. Each individual person has a particular regard to such parameters according to context, circumstances, experience and understandings. Social convention affects the way adults use their skills of communicative engagement, compartmentalising them for use at certain times, under certain circumstances or in certain contexts. As children grow up, we apply a vast array of socially constructed understandings about communicative interchanges such as: adults tell children and children listen to adults; eye-contact signifies engagement; moving out of an unfinished communication signifies insolence and interrupting is rude. Special Time is asking adults to return to trying to engage with a child from a child's perspective and to make meaning of a communicative encounter based on that child's experience and communicative behaviours. We ask adults to participate in activities that they may find embarrassing but their children do not. Adults find it embarrassing because they are in a non-standard social circumstance. Special Time is asking adults to concentrate, at this point in time, on co-construction and to temporarily suspend many socially constructed notions of what a communicative exchange 'should' consist of.

Special Time: how inclusive is it?

During the 1990s and particularly in the latter half of the decade, a central tenet of government policy was the promotion of social inclusion. The moves to develop inclusive educational provision can be seen as part of the government's initiatives to reduce segregation and exclusion across and within communities, as well as being a human rights issue.

The term 'inclusion' has almost replaced 'integration' in current parlance. Integration was formerly used to describe the placement of children with special educational needs in mainstream schools (geographical/locational integration). Integration can be defined as the provision of 'additional arrangements' to enable settings to admit certain children with particular needs but where the setting itself remains essentially unchanged. 'Integration in its most negative connotation stands for integration by location, whilst providing a watered-down variant of the regular curriculum' (Pijl *et al.* 1997: 2). Inclusion is characterised by a much more radical approach, going beyond the location of pupils in mainstream schools based on pupils' individual disabilities and towards developing 'a philosophy of acceptance and about providing a framework within which all children (regardless of the provenance of their difficulty at school) can be valued equally, treated with respect and provided with equal opportunities at school' (Thomas 1997: 103).

Oliver (1996), describing some of the differences between integration and inclusion, conceptualised them as the interplay between state and process, acceptance and cele-bration, tolerance and valuing, normality and diversity. While definitions of inclusion will involve various moral, political, social and educational aims and assumptions (Clarke *et al.* 1997; Sebba and Ainscow 1996), the basic demands are that in all settings 'every child is welcomed, whatever their degree of disability or learning difficulty' (Alderson 1999: 4). As a society, however, we still tend to seek out difference and use it to exclude people from certain aspects of that society. We carry with us a negative model of difference. To be different is seen as lacking in ability to be the same. As we enter the twenty-first century major barriers to inclusive education still have to be addressed as we labour with what Clough and Corbett (2000) have termed the psycho-medical model which essentially sees the disabled individual as being 'in deficit'. Recently I asked a group of mature students the question 'What is autism?' The stu-dents were beginning their first unit on a Masters Degree in Autism. They either work with, or are parents of, children/young people with autism. Their responses were expansive but interestingly, until gently prompted by my colleague, the students had intuitively listed a set of negative characteristics. If we look at part of the students' list and apply the descriptions to the behaviour of a 9-month-old baby, they would perhaps fit.

People with autistic spectrum disorders are likely to have:

- Different perspective of the world (*we* assume this to be so)
- Inability to accept nuances
- Unpredictable behaviours
- Difficulty with flexibility of thought
- Inability to pick up social cues
- Theory of mind difficulties
- Difficulties with abstract thought processes
- Single-mindedness
- Prediction difficulties that can, for example, affect perceptions of danger
- Isolated skills
- A need for routine
- Problems with generalisation

If I had asked the students to describe a 9-month-old baby, this would not perhaps have been the list of characteristics they would have offered. We seem to hold a set of nor-mative descriptions constructed by both psychologists and society that have become what Burman (1994) terms 'naturalised prescriptions'. These offer us a vernacular measure against which society tends to decide what is acceptable at a given age, at a given time and in a given context: 'definitions of childhood are relational, they exist in relation to definitions of adults, of mothers and fathers, of families, of the State' (ibid.: 59). It could be said that a 'Special Time' group that removes children from their regular setting is a clear example of segregation and exclusion. Inclusion, however, is a much more complex notion than geographical location. While being educated together is a tangible symbol of being together, developing inclusive practice that enables everyone to engage with one another, to socialise and learn together involves problem-solving, commitment and vision. 'Inclusive schools are diverse problem solving organisations with a common mission that emphasises learning for all students' (Rouse and Florian 1996). The Special Time group aimed to help both clarify the abilities and needs of the children and to support the adults in being more aware of their own skills, abilities and frames of reference. Without negating the enormous needs of the children, Special Time values what they bring to the group. It utilises the abilities of professionals/practitioners, parents and children to develop a functionally communicative environment, both within the group, and beyond. Working with the child's playgroup/nursery is fundamental to developing a wider commitment to accessible services. These services must be accessible not just in terms of enabling a child to physically 'be there', but ensuring that the child is able to engage, in a meaningful way, in both the learning and socialising that go on in early years settings. Special Time is a joint venture between practitioners, families and children. It is about understanding and learning together as part of a much wider process.

Special Time is not 'inclusive' in terms of our ideal vision. It removes children from their settings, however temporarily, and both the children and their settings lose a learning opportunity, even though they gain another. We struggle with the dominant values and organisational systems of our time and how we work at the boundaries of those systems to try and stretch them out; to be more flexible and innovative. Our current notions of education and access to education facilities and curricula are constantly being challenged but building new understandings of what an education system can offer, and how it could offer learning opportunities that are truly for all, is complex. It necessitates looking at and interrogating our own beliefs and understandings in a consciously explicit manner. It necessitates reframing the social construction of difference as deficit into a recognition of the gains to be made from recognising and using the skills we have and developing new understandings together. It involves knowing that this is not going to be easy, but being confident that we can do it.

Conclusion

This investigation into Special Time has helped clarify some of the skills that adults (and children), parents and practitioners, use daily and intuitively. It shapes the understanding and use of adult communication skills into a pragmatic and consciously focused approach that is constantly tested against new observations and reflections on both child and adult behaviours.

Special Time takes a micro-perspective on the co-construction of a functional communicative engagement. The multiple reciprocal relationships of communication are peeled back to reveal an interplay between the complexity of communication and achieving a direct, honed down, language/talking system that offers functional interchanges between two parties. The aim is to reduce complexities in a strategic manner and to provide a directness that unhooks impulse, social custom and habit from practice within an analytical framework for developing mutual understandings. Special Time offers an opportunity to work on co-construction, to develop a strategic engagement that addresses the interaction between individual and socially prescribed notions of communication such as culture/tradition and the application of knowledge. It offers an opportunity to consider the interplay between consciously and tacitly held knowledge, complex language and direct engagement and ambiguity and clarity. Special Time is a continuous cycle of framing and reframing our knowledge and use of that knowledge in the light of what is presented by the communicative situation in which we find ourselves.

Two encounters in a foreign land

A woman on vacation in France wants to buy some brown bread for her family. She has a little 'holiday French' and practises the sentence 'Du pain, s'il vous plâit' [some bread please]. When she enters the shop it is full of the most amazing variety of bread, sticks, loaves, buns, plaits and more. As she takes in the sights and enjoys the warm, doughy atmosphere, the woman is asked by the shop assistant what she would like 'Qu'est-ce que vous voulez, madame?' The woman quickly gathers her wits, guesses what question she has been asked and says her phrase 'Du pain, s'il vous plâit'. The shop assistant asks what kind of bread madame would like. 'Un pain seigle, peut-être, pain de campagne, un pain complet?' Not prepared for her phrase to be questioned, and not understanding the question, the woman is a little thrown. She pauses and smiles as she tries to make sense of what has been said to her. Just as she thinks she has understood and perhaps could respond, the assistant, keen to help, says 'Vous voulez une ficelle, peut-être?' [Perhaps you would like a thin white bread stick?] Now the woman is losing her confidence. She is a little flustered and avoids eye contact with the shop assistant in an attempt to prevent more words coming her way. She scans the shelves of bread and then, seeing a reasonably large baguette, points to it. It is not brown, but now any large amount of bread will do. She points to it.

'Ahh,' says the shop assistant, 'une grande baguette.' [A large baguette.] 'Oui,' says the woman and hurriedly puts a selection of notes and coins on the counter. The shop assistant wraps the large white baguette, takes the correct money giving the woman the change, smiles and bids her 'Au revoir'. The woman smiles, looks down and leaves the shop. She feels frustrated because she did not make herself understood; she had not managed to buy any of the wonderful brown bread on offer. She has left the shop with bread she did not really want and without the vocabulary necessary to get the correct bread next time.

Another woman on vacation in France wants to buy bread. She finds a bread shop and enters, marvelling at the amazing variety of bread, sticks, loaves, buns, plaits and more displayed before her. As she takes in the sights and enjoys the warm, doughy atmosphere the woman is asked by the shop assistant what she would like, 'Qu'est-ce que vous voulez, madame?' The woman doesn't understand the words, but guesses the meaning of the question. She surveys the breads on offer and chooses one by pointing at some interesting-looking brown bread. The shop assistant follows her pointing finger and says, 'Un pain complet?' [brown bread?] 'Oui,' says the woman and repeats the words 'Pain complet.' The shop assistant smiles and says the words again, 'Pain complet', as she puts the bread into the bag. The woman repeats the words in her head, now associating them with this loaf of bread. As she puts her money on the counter, the shop assistant takes a 10 franc piece, holds it up and with a smile says 'Dix francs.' 'Dix francs,' repeats the woman.

The next day the woman went into another bread shop. Again there was lots of bread but she couldn't see what she wanted. With a big smile she said to the assistant, 'Un pain complet, s'il vous plâit.' The shop assistant went into the back room and came out with un pain complet fresh from the oven. Both women smiled. 'Dix francs,' said the shop assistant, and the woman happily rummaged in her purse for the required coin.

CHAPTER 7

Horse Whispering for Humans: A Sensitive Approach to Behaviour Difficulties

Marysia Holubecki

Supposing you take one horse, wild or not, and 'armed' with only a length of rope, to act as an extension of your arm, you take that horse into a round pen. You then, standing in the centre 'chase' the horse away using your body language; you square up to the horse, wave your arms and make firm eye contact. Horses will flee this predatory stance as a matter of instinct. You continue to persevere with this attitude, and make them change direction. They will gradually, as you do nothing 'worse' start to listen to you. You will know this because they will lower their heads and snort at the ground; the ear nearest to you will turn in towards you. You start to change your body language, you relax your stance, turn sideways onto the horse and lessen your eye contact. The horse will pick up on this. When they actually start chewing and licking (honestly!) you know that they are starting to listen and think. You are asking the horse to join up with you; you are telling him that there is nothing to be frightened of. He is thinking that he'd like to be safe. These signals and responses are, in my experience, remarkably predictable. You then turn your back completely on the horse. They will stop if they haven't already. You back up to them, look down, lower your eyes. When you reach the horse you may reach out behind you and touch them on the shoulder or neck or forehead, keeping your back to the horse and eyes down. Then, after a few moments, walk in any direction you wish, slowly, and the horse will be following you! This does 'work' and with intermittent games or reminders it lasts over time.

Pat Parelli, an exponent of intelligent horsemanship, also emphasizes the importance of horses learning much of this through play and games. Are these not instantly ideas to be translated and transferred to young people? Games such as advance/retreat; chase and stop; pulling and pushing and stopping as soon as the right response happens. It is probably no coincidence that these have the same 'rules' as many a successful playground game!

(Marysia in conversation)

It was while discussing the subject of stress, among teachers and children, and of the vicious circles this generates, that I commented on a parallel with animals, in particular horses, and how they behave differently whether under stress or not. The notion of horse whispering in relation to humans had been discussed by myself with colleagues and friends for years, long before Monty Robert's *Horse-sense for Humans*. Monty Roberts (1997) says that good trainers can hear horses talking to them; great trainers can hear them whisper. It is about language (communication), listening, leadership, love, and a respectful partnership based on these, that allows performance, a light and easy way of working and the opportunity to teach or rather to learn. With animals, unless you want only minimal achievement and that through fear, bullying and force, however nicely dressed it is, you will *not* have a relationship of performance unless you have a trusting and open relationship. With a horse this is quite obvious to see, as it is the difference between him accepting you as a leader/partner or continuing to be a flight animal performing certain learnt habits, some good and some bad, but all out of fear.

Needless to say with humans, the story becomes more complicated, as we fundamentally are a complex mix of flight and fight animals, along with all of the associated behaviours and emotional responses when placed in particular sets of circumstances. Nonetheless there are significant parallels.

I am interested in the applicability of this theory to the mainstream classroom, not simply to those with difficult behaviour, but as a way of contemplating and understanding the quality of daily interactions, and the possible implications and consequences of language styles, both verbal and non-verbal, with all children, although undoubtedly the difficult ones are most noticeable.

Horses, like all animals, will try to communicate, naturally with other horses but also with humans. These attempts will be open to interpretation and indeed misinterpretation. Horses in turn will interpret attempts at communication by humans. But they will only be able to read the signals in terms that their language allows. If the human signals are interpreted as threatening, demanding, predatory, aggressive or any other negative stance, then stress will increase and some fairly set patterns of behaviour will ensue. Behaviours such as pulling, knocking over, running away, rearing, kicking, will be defined as undesirable when they are entirely natural in the circumstances . . . and in turn will increase stress in the human who will be likely to incite use of yet more of the initially faulty language/signals, and so on . . .

And so I thought it might well be the experience for some of our teachers and children who, for myriad confusing reasons, are effectively, or rather ineffectively, speaking a different language. The suggestion goes something like this: Imagine a young person, possibly with underlying difficulties ranging from mild autism, semantic-pragmatic issues, poor or impoverished social use of language due to environment and background or learning difficulty, depression, very polarised learning style, to other possibly unrecognised speech and language impairment, who outwardly displays challenging behaviour. The child is probably under a good deal of stress already and suffering a cocktail of fear of failure, anger, unhappiness, confusion, frustration, inability to cope. The already generally stressed teacher may misinterpret or interpret the child's verbal and non-verbal language as unhelpful, unfriendly, antagonistic, arrogant, ungrateful, or disrespectful. The adult may mirror this or even feel that it 'deserves' similar in response. And whether the interpretation was right and the reaction deserved or not within the education situation, this, I would argue, only further increases the stress of both and is likely to damage further relationships and to encourage more of the similar kinds of communication. The downward spiral begins.

Now, in the case of horses, there is a way of turning this situation around and approaching the whole notion of communication from the standpoint of the *need* to have as a starting point a common language. It would be very difficult for a horse to acquire an understanding of our rules of language, so, to move forward, we must understand its reactions. This isn't giving in or losing control to the horse; indeed, it keeps control for the human, simply in a different way. Similarly, with children, I believe, we must at least try to communicate with them in a way that they cannot help but see as positive. We need to be aware of how our attempts at communicating are really interpreted. (This isn't either about being soft and not having standards or boundaries, it is something much more subtle than that.) Indeed, we as practitioners and adults need to be able to interpret a young person's behavioural signals in a sympathetic, understanding and yet impersonal way. For example, their body language, sentence length and structure, ability to take turns, eye contact, etc. might be poor. Critically, though, we should ask the question, why? What is the intentionality of the actions? What are the reasons for them? Maybe, they are not intended to annoy but arise because of anger, frustration, unhappiness? Perhaps we need actively to resist the possibly subconscious response of modelling or mirroring similar responses back. Of course as professionals we all try to do exactly this, in theory, that is! Although there will not be room for an in-depth study of the associated and relevant issues, this does not invalidate a brief foray into the world of horse whispering for humans!

Stress and its effects

There is no doubt and no wonder that teachers are stressed. Difficult behaviours in the young people they work with are often identified, on stress questionnaires carried out with staff, as an issue of particular note. And stress breeds stress. Being stressed makes it more difficult to be calm, measured, thoughtful, generous, reflective, helpful, unemotional, even professional, and impersonal. And the behaviour that initially triggered and justified some response escalates. Some of the following quotations may indicate some of the stresses to which I am referring. The examples are real and in the main are fairly negative snapshots of interactions. They are anonymous and uncontextualised. However, that is not to say that I am being overly critical, or making generalisations or saying there are not positive interactions in greater numbers. It is rather an observation of human nature at work under stress or when working in the dark as many teachers are with unidentified problems and little or no training in how to work with particular difficulties. And I think in all honesty we have all been there or somewhere near in thought, word or deed. That simply makes us all human. But it still does not make it helpful for either party. And possibly contrary to popular myth, this group of individuals is often much *more sensitive* to verbal and non-verbal messages than others, waiting, from experience perhaps, for something to be hurtful, confusing, and contradictory. Changing their experience and expectation of communication is therefore not easy.

Some real examples of unhelpful patterns of communication

After the teacher has told the whole class to come out to the desk for help, a child with learning difficulties goes up a few minutes later and the question is, 'Now what are you doing out of your seat?' This is confusing enough if you have learning difficulties but what if Aspergers is an issue? Or semantic-pragmatic difficulties or if you are angry or unhappy, but lack the emotional literacy to cope with these feelings?

Child: I liked my old school better.
Teacher: I wish you would go back there.

Teacher: Don't be so stupid, I don't want to speak to you. You know, I cannot trust you.

Teacher: It is no wonder you don't have any friends.

Teacher: This school is a much nicer place without you.

Teacher: Are you deaf?

Teacher: Is there something wrong with your brain?

Teacher: How dare you swear in front of me, you filthy mouthed swine?

Teacher: I am bigger and better than you.

Teacher: We just want you to be normal.

Teacher: I cannot help you if you can't tell me what is wrong.

Teacher: Why can't you behave?

Teacher: The rest of us will not start until you have the decency to sit down.

Teacher: Look at me when I am talking to you.

There are also many, some very understandable, human and even amusing descriptors of behaviours that are not specific enough to be helpful and may not indicate real difficulties, e.g. temperamental, unfriendly, has to be the centre of attention, disturbed, hyper, unkind, always in trouble, mad as a fish, he /she has something wrong, a gene missing, is just like his brother and does my head in.

So this opening or motivational scenario is one which, as a professional working with children of all ages with identified emotional and behavioural difficulties, I see with worrying regularity and hear about from members of my team daily. Individuals are often referred with descriptions of the difficulties they present to staff in schools and of the types of behaviour they are exhibiting. Often, there will be some indication that it is something that the staff should not have to put up with and that the child's manner and attitude leave much to be desired. Indeed, it is often stated that the child is stubborn, confrontational, difficult, impossible to talk to or reason with or will avoid eye contact completely or stare or be silent or run away. Basically, a picture of unhelpful, negative, destructive communication, which will do nothing except possibly further harm to the relationship, if indeed one exists!

Now, instantly of interest to me, is the fact that I have never heard any staff *volunteer* information about the way they feel they have been interacting and reacting in these situations, i.e. that they are *part* of the picture. This is not to say that the problems are not mainly with the child but I do not believe that this is the end of the story. Nor am I saying that teachers should have to put up with being spoken to like this or treated like that. But, then, how are the young people being treated? Does the single fact that the young people have problems, challenging behaviour and treat teachers in an unacceptable manner in fact mean that reciprocating these features is helpful or right? And yes, I do mean even within the current climate of pressure regarding academic achievement, the implementation of the National Curriculum, and the 31 or more other children. These factors do not seem to prevent at least acknowledgement that any other Special Educational Needs child has individual rights and needs, so why is this case any different? Perhaps it is because this, more than any other area, involves feelings of resentment, personal attack, persecution, and highlights more than anything the subsequent feelings of stress, doubt, resistance, defensiveness, anger, paranoia, threat, fear and being out of one's depth. Think how many parallels there are with the way in which the child may well be feeling. And yet teachers are supposed to be trained to be the leaders; the professional, responsible, calm party who has the role of guiding and leading, without more outdated notions of authority or control.

What we may need to look for is an improved or altered social context or attitude within schools that relieves stress through understanding and enhanced communication. This, I suggest, can in a very small way be addressed by another look at, and perhaps a new perspective on, the nature of communication and the need for a common understanding of language used. We cannot get rid of all stresses. There is intrinsic stress in real difficulties experienced by young people and it would seem that educational stress is fairly entrenched, as are long practised negative behaviour patterns. However, we can possibly cope with it differently and, by doing so, get rid of some degree of anxiety.

I would like us to be able to talk more about how relationships and interactions *feel* and for that in itself to carry weight – not for it to be simply a sum of the parts of discourse, which like the most accurate description of secondary qualities of an object do not yet give us the real sense of what it is *like* for a person to experience something. It does not mean that it is not valid for that person to have that feeling or for him to lack accuracy or expertise in sensing it. We are all *expert* in how we feel when in interaction with others, and I would argue that teachers need to be in touch with the subjective art of communication. Instead, everyone wants a pack or a handout or some strategies and skills. People often just want to know how to do something, not always why or how it works, which is why I am against scripts and plans and strategies to train emotional intelligence at the outset. While I appreciate the security they afford and the resemblance to the delivery of the rest of the curriculum, I doubt their effectiveness without engagement on a more subjective and individual, personal level. Otherwise, you can get the case of professionals *speaking the speak*, but not really translating scripts into genuine behaviour and attitude change.

Using the model of working with horses may be one such way into this delicate, hugely subjective and personal, yet essential area. That is, looking at the quality of inter-actions between children and adults where behaviour is an issue, and the implications and effects of the *quality* of those interactions on the resulting behaviour and relation-ship.

Horse whispering: showing respect, relationship and leadership

The whole notion of horse whispering or intelligent horsemanship is not new, nor are its parallels with human communication. If we go back approximately 100 years, horses had a much higher standing within the workings of society. They were still a luxury but were perhaps much more essential to life than other luxuries. Accordingly, in the main, they were loved, respected, needed. The relationship had to be positive to be success-ful and so the essential components of love (respect), language (communication), lead-ership were ever present, and those who ignored them and attempted to bully a relationship never achieved a lightness or ease of working relationship. They never achieved partnership. More time and effort and patience were allowed for with less of the modern anxiety about results, now or yesterday, and targets to be met.

I believe that in the same way that this way of working has been lost to horseman-ship during much of the twentieth century, until the school of Monty Roberts and others, so have the same fundamental positive features disappeared from much of our communication with each other. I wonder whether there is less time, opportunity and enthusiasm for conversation these days. And does the National Literacy Strategy encourage non-specific, spontaneous conversations? Is conversation no longer seen as the most valued way to engage? In schools, was it always the case that communication styles had some unfortunate patterns, but that this was somehow balanced by conver-sations that happened in other places? Also, that somehow it did not mean automatic loss of role and respect which seems to be one of the main issues that teachers have within school currently: the tension between role, respect, authority, relationship. Now some may argue quite persuasively that love, language, leadership and partnership were not present in the communication styles of, for example, Victorian schools. Maybe something else was making up for this, and/or issues of poor behaviour due to poor relationship were contained or masked by different and now unacceptable practices. Or maybe good communication has always happened more by accident between those who already possessed enough of the requisite sensitivity.

Exponents of horse whispering (communicating with horses) talk about horses being naturally flight animals and that there are some parallels with humans who are clearly a confusing mixture of both flight and fight. Often, if put under pressure, they will run or they may oppose pressure by barging, reciprocating invasion of space or by applying pressure back. Does this bear any resemblance to classroom situations where teachers 'make' children uncomfortable by applying pressure, invading space, confront-ing with the resulting reaction being, 'I am out of here' or a push back physically or ver-bally? If, however, we signal or ask and keep the parties feeling comfortable, we can often achieve results that feel easy or even agreeable. We make it easy for the horse or person to do the 'right' thing, which is not, for horses in training or people in society, often the natural or innate response, just the appropriate one. As perhaps the best known proponent of horse whispering, Monty Roberts (1997), says:

> In most work situations, we are asking humans to make choices that are equally unnatural, equally threatening . . . It is not natural to follow a rigid set of rules and guidelines and to have our security and future in the hands of people we do not know or perhaps do not even like. Many of the behaviours that employees resent in employers (and vice versa) are simply the result of natural resistance to unnatural conditions. One of the goals in human–human join-up then, is to create through communication and behaviour, situations where the satisfaction of co-operation outweighs the negative reaction to unnatural condition (p. 31).

Horse whispering suggests that horses, when engaged with love, language and leadership, can learn to trust and feel comfortable (and comfort for horses can mean being left alone); they can, then, respond more appropriately to pressure, i.e. to move in an appropriate or the required direction, rather than resisting it or running from it. Therefore the horse whispering school would suggest that building a relationship by forcing, directing, even 'bullying' will result in a poor relationship whereas a relationship built on comfort and ease will attain the opposite.

Things may not work the first, second or third time but then a good horse-trainer will automatically look for faults in the signals, not in the horse. Teachers and riders often share a sense of injustice, when they have made every effort but still to no avail. They have not been unkind or cruel, they care. It is difficult to be 'mature' enough not to take affront when clearly this caring is still not enough, or more likely the wrong tack altogether.

Joining in partnership: building a relationship based on a common understanding of 'language'

Unlike horses who are flight animals, humans can either be flight or fight animals, because of our make-up we are constantly deciding whether we are prey or predator. 'Join-up' provides a third option in the form of partnership. It is possible to create a partnership with a horse using language it understands based on trust and respect and on an understanding of its behaviour in the wild. This is possible with wild or trained animals, regardless of how experienced the person involved is, as long as the process is followed accurately. It is possible to harness their natural instincts as flight animals to relax and perform when in their comfort zones. For a horse, a comfort zone is one where pressure is non-existent, body language is passive and gentle eye contact is made. And contrary to popular human opinion, horses have to 'learn' to like being patted or smiled at, in the sense that in their natural language these are 'danger signals or threats'. We could learn from this that we possibly should not make assumptions about what a comfort zone is for a child whether they are autistic, have emotional and behavioural difficulties, or have a very polarised working style/personality, etc.

So I come back to the description of 'join-up' which opens this chapter, with the underlying notion that some form of human-to-human join-up is also possible. Certainly in terms of body language, most counselling skills training and anger management training would suggest exactly this (see Faupel *et al.* 1998; MacGrath 1998). Indeed, work in the field of emotional literacy is surely in tune with this (see Sharp 2001).

Conclusion

Possibly there is a need to save the horse-whispering analogy from whimsiness or an over-romanticised mental picture of Robert Redford, or indeed any notion of crankiness, magic, trickery or simply an art reserved for the enlightened or gifted few. Surely we all have the potential to be enlightened? I can just hear, 'Well it may be OK/easy for him/in those circumstances/with horses not children.' You may be asking, 'Does this work? Has she tried it?' With horses, yes, with humans as best I can. We are only human after all.

There is no set formula, not even one like the staged training of horses in this method. There are probably too many variables we genuinely are not in control of. I certainly do not envisage children being chased around the playground and then allowed to come back in trust and respect, *not* because I think it would not work but because I cannot see it fitting in (yet?). But certainly the ability, whether innate, learned, or a mix of both, to communicate in this way with children, I see every day by members of support services and with many teachers. And, yes, this is possibly just a reworking, a different perspective on the age-old fundamentals of respect and earning that respect. But it is long overdue. Especially as it is less and less supported by systems and structures within education, the home, and wider society, and more and more up to the individual teacher to face up to the challenge. So maybe this is a little bit of support for that challenge even if it is only moral support.

This challenge is made more so with the inclusion agenda, and the raising achievement agenda. It is about a change in attitude and understanding, not about having a script or quoting a piece of research; indeed, it is about knowledge from experience and we all can have that. As Tom Billington says:

> *'Knowledge is a mix of intelligence and intuition' (2000: 117).*

⁕⁂ ⚜ ⁂⁕

A conversational story about a puddle

Sheila: I went in to see one of our little boys in reception who was causing great problems for the teacher, because he always got his feet wet in the puddles in the yard (it was one of these yards that had puddles) . . . and like a lot of children with language/communication difficulties, he loved water and jumping in the puddles, so . . .

he was in dreadful trouble for getting his shoes and socks and everything . . . even his trousers wet every day . . . and I went in on one occasion to find the little boy sitting in the cloakroom all by himself, with his head down, looking absolutely dejected . . . he couldn't tell me what was the matter . . . but he was sort of pointing to the cubby hole underneath where his shoes and socks were put away . . . and he was sitting in his bare feet.

So afterwards, I went to see the teacher who said in annoyance, 'Oh, do you know what he's done today? Do you know what he's done? Can you believe what he's done today! He took his shoes off and he went out in his socks and deliberately jumped in the puddles! He had promised me he wouldn't get his shoes wet. He promised me he wouldn't get his shoes wet and look what he's done!'

If she had taken the trouble to look at that child's face, she would have seen the puzzlement. I saw it as soon as I looked at him: the puzzlement on his face . . . as if to say 'she told me not to get my shoes wet and I didn't, so why is she cross?'

Marysia: I do think it comes back to lack of understanding. This whole business about theory of mind is not something that people have actually considered . . . thought about . . . discussed for themselves. It's like emotional intelligence; it's like social construction of meaning; it's like cognitive behaviour theory; it's like any number of things that seem to have bypassed a lot of people who are actually actively teaching.

Sheila: Yes, it's absolutely fundamental, if we're going to understand kids with communication difficulties, to look through the child's eyes.

CHAPTER 8

Support and Stabilisers: Addressing Anxiety in Reading Failure

What happens when we ride a bicycle might form the basis of a highly technical lecture by a physicist . . . But if we sat a novice bicycle rider down and explained the skills involved we would not be helping him to ride. What we actually do is sit him on the bicycle and provide support – we hold on until he is ready to go it alone. (I believe we can apply just such a teaching method to children learning to read.)

(Martin 1989: 23)

This chapter considers ways of re-engaging children in the pleasures of reading and writing stories, children who by the age of eight are oppressed by their failure to learn to read and whose parents consequently feel burdened and anxious. I shall be describing a home/school approach to reading failure that seeks to support anxious children rather than to champion any particular literacy strategy. Since so many young children seem to learn with little overt help, there is a sense of panic, for parents and children alike, when reading doesn't 'click' for them. Perhaps our concern in this country to press early literacy inevitably creates these 'failures'.

Anxiety makes for maladaptive strategies like wild guessing, panic-stricken scanning or a desperate reliance on memorisation. So, dealing with anxiety, rather than adopting remedial measures, becomes the focus of my attention. I have revived old-fashioned approaches like paired reading to involve parents, but more important than the method is *how* it is mediated. The quality of the relationship and contextual conditions are what matters.

It is well documented that children with specific speech and language difficulties are likely to be numbered among these failures (Bishop and Adams 1990; Snowling 2000; Stackhouse 2000). Rather than strive to pinpoint the precise difficulties that face the diverse children under the specific language impairment umbrella, I present a holistic approach, which can *include* very different children in one intervention. The paired reading approach was first used in a clinical setting with stammerers, and its supportive voice helped children maintain the flow of speech. It reduced the pressure to talk as a solo performer and relaxation healed the hiatus in speech production. It is likely, therefore, to be of use for anxious children. For them all, anxiety can escalate in

He knows all the children in this group, so he could tell me the names to put on the cards. He can now tell me that he is not feeling well, or that he played football, and I can understand his sentences. (Parent)

pressured home reading sessions or when performing in embarrassing classroom contexts.

The approach to reading described later was first practised in the 1980s before the advent of the National Curriculum. Like a river in a limestone region, the importance of the child making sense has gone underground for a decade but is resurfacing. I am hopeful that my approach has a renewed chance of being implemented in the current climate with its reassertion of the value of social construction of meanings and the importance of motivating relationships. It had faded temporarily from view, overtaken by the strong political thrust to promote the learning of skills. The unacknowledged metaphor of 'delivery' of the curriculum in intervention 'packages' can be (but does not have to be) at odds with the bicycling metaphor which opens this chapter. This metaphor shows the importance of learning to read by *doing* it in a supportive climate. Reading is not about applying isolated skills, but about a dynamic interaction with text. You cannot train visual perception or auditory discrimination and expect these skills necessarily to transfer to the reading process.

This is the same point as was made about language learning: learning receptive or expressive skills, or acquiring vocabulary outside the zone of use, can lead to a parroting practice. In the literacy domain, the equivalent to parroting is barking at print: in both cases, skills are acquired without comprehension. Skill-driven models are inadequate to describe the dynamic of engaging in dialogue or the dynamic of interacting with text *and* reading out loud *to* someone. Both encounters are inevitably charged with emotion, whether of pain or pleasure predominantly. Anxiety can disrupt any scheme. Not being able to make sense of an activity enjoyed by others is agitating and alienating.

I have frequently been urged to write up my rationale and findings, but have been unwilling to subject anxious children, whom teachers have screened as non-readers, to psychometric tests to establish a baseline in the empirical research mode. A pre-test which the children could not manage was likely to set negative perceptions of the forthcoming Special Time. Attitudes to reading, however, were clearly discovered by asking children to choose their favourite pastimes from pictures (including things like washing-up and tidying bedrooms) and noting if in any combination of picture choices, children chose the book option. They were also given chances to identify with children pictured as busily occupied, and the child engaged with a book was not chosen. After the intervention, it was easy to see that avoidance was replaced by a desire to share books.

Ideological tangles

Unfortunately reading is still entangled with teaching ideologies and books are still written to 'implicate the child-centred, whole-word methods of reading instruction in England as a decisive factor in the decline of England's standard' (Macmillan 1997: 16). New 'revolutionary' approaches to the teaching of reading blame failure on faulty teaching (McGuinness 1998). Both of these authors seek to 'expose the gap' between practice and research findings. Empirical research, they claim, has overwhelmingly proved that phoneme awareness is at the heart of successful reading acquisition

Table 8.1   Different methods of teaching reading

Whole-word methods	Phonological methods
Meaning emphasis (non-code)	Code emphasis
Look-and-say (i.e. *single-word memorisation, words memorised as whole visual units*)	Direct, structured teaching of phonics in systematic way
Language-experience	Deliberate sequence of activities (i.e. first the alphabetic principle then blending)
Integrated reading and writing (i.e. *memorisation of personal sets of words used in individualised writing activities*)	Exposure to specially designed phonic texts.
Shared book reading	
Paired reading	
Apprenticeship model	
Whole-language methods using 'real books'	
Attractive texts with *natural* language	
Progressive, child-centred	**Teacher-as-director**
Teacher-as-facilitator	**Disciplined and attentive pupils**
Noisy, uncontrolled classrooms	

(Goswami and Bryant 1990). Whereas McGuinness recognises that politics have tangled with theory, and that too much 'energy and rhetoric is expended on blaming political parties of the right and left for absolutely everything that's wrong with society' (1998: 361), Macmillan, while purporting to be 'even-handed', cannot disguise her ideological stance, and she drags reading back into the political arena. She perpetuates rigid polarisations with the two camps characterised (or caricatured) in Table 8.1.

I have emboldened the parts in Table 8.1 that bring in an ideological, political dimension, to highlight the difficulty of separating the teaching of reading skills from beliefs on how learning should be mediated. Being a humanistic psychologist myself, I see mutual respect as the basis of child-centredness, and would argue that 'noisy, uncontrolled classrooms' contradict this tenet. I recognise my underlying belief system, and want to reassemble the elements in the columns in Table 8.1 so that there is no longer a rigid alliance between a belief and a method, between child-centredness and whole-word ways. Until this is done, we are in danger of wasting valuable time and research money to prove a viewpoint or to blame opponents. What I should like to do is erase this artificial partition, and re-group elements which I see as promoting literacy. For example, I would like to bring 'paired reading' across the divide, and promote it as an excellent multi-sensory approach, and, as such, useful to the dyslexia lobby, which tends to espouse the phonics camp.

Also, it is no longer valid to separate visual from auditory senses as if they were independent systems. Early perceptual development urges a more integrated sensory system, and highlights the amazing fact that the baby turns to look at what she hears. So, a purely logographic recognition habit (of the look-and-say type), which relies solely on remembering words as if they were pictures, is bound to be insufficient. Yet it is equally one-sided to isolate phonemic awareness in an activity that requires the eye to scan marks on paper! I agree that the timing and sequence of activities are crucial, and I adopt ideas taken from the psychology of physical skill: learned sub-skills combine with practice to become an automatic function. Hence the bicycling analogy.

I am not going for 'mixed' methods to pour oil on troubled waters. Possibly those who advocate mixed methods do so to avoid sterile debate with its covert ideology. For some, since no one as yet has come up with a resounding answer, the safest ploy is to put a bit of everything into the mixture to guard one's back from attack from one side or the other. I recognise the dangers of such evasion. For me lack of commitment and direction is as likely to be the reason for failure as is a disregard for research findings. Child-centred approaches have suffered from *laissez-faire* style, a lack of mediation masquerading as respect for individual freedom. To be truly child-centred is to be strongly focused, attentive and rigorously evaluative.

Giving time and close attention to pupils can be as powerful as any programme. When there is loud acclaim for a structured phonic approach as the answer, the magic ingredient could be the careful organisation or focused attention, and not the phonic diet alone. Even the researchers who have correlated phonemic awareness with successful reading performance understand that this does not indicate causation and cannot provide evidence for teaching a 'phonemic awareness' programme as a proven solution.

> We have had to come to two uncomfortable conclusions – uncomfortable, at any rate, for the authors of a book about phonological awareness and reading. The first is that there is little direct evidence that children who are learning to read do rely on letter-sound relationships to help them read words. The second is that there is a great deal of evidence that these young children take easily and naturally to reading words in other ways. (Goswami and Bryant 1990: 46)

So, rather than perpetuate arid debate, I would like to propose a new synthesis of elements in the reading interaction that might be at the heart of successful learning.

Short Period Reading INTervention (SPRINT)

Dealing with anxiety became for me the way into success rather than a slavish following of a method. This led to projects called SPRINT (Short Period Reading INTervention). Complementary effort was made by parents and teachers for a period of six weeks (coordinated by myself as the educational psychologist working in both contexts).

Parental involvement

Parents were introduced to the paired reading approach (for materials see Topping 1988 and for a review of research see Topping and Lindsay 1992). It was not the method itself that sufficed, but how it was put across. There has been too much time wasted in pointless contentions about the mechanics of the approach – e.g. how many seconds to wait before giving the word – instead of focus on mediation style. My project took pains not to train parents in a procedure ordained from on high by the experts, but to solicit their cooperation in a joint venture which accorded instinctively with their own feelings about reading. Whereas I have had trouble persuading teachers about reading this way, very few parents have quarrelled with it. It is an extension of their own practice of reading stories to their children without fear of interfering with school's expertise. Knowing they are helping not hindering removes their inhibiting anxiety. Their role is clarified: they are not trying to be surrogate teachers but remain as parents enjoying time with their children. Many claim that cuddling up to read improved relationships as well as attainments.

So, how was this done? Children who were not readers by age eight and who were deemed to be anxious were chosen by schools. Their parents were invited to a group get-together before any intervention took place in the classroom. Parents found they were not the only ones for whom hearing reading at home as directed by school was a frustrating affair. They shared their annoyance and despair at their futile attempts to drag unwilling children to set books. Often the same book was the diet for weeks on end, and any interest it might have sparked had long since died. Often parents felt obliged to carry on and made up entries in the home-school book, in fear of censure. Slavish adherence to given pages without thought of story continuity was frequent. Almost without exception, children attended fleetingly, and bribery and threat loomed large. Forcing compliance achieved little but bad feeling and confrontation. Children had become adept at evasion and bargaining. There were lies about lost books and 'What teacher says'. The degree to which children disowned the process was shown in lost and damaged books, a refusal to look at the page or even to share holding a book with an adult. Enjoying stories did not figure.

Then, after talking in pairs, we pooled some of the bafflement that parents felt about reading behaviour. Every time, the same wonderings came up:

> *Why does she know the word on one page and has no idea on the next?*
> *Why can he read the long words and not the little ones?*
> *She guesses and looks at the picture instead of looking at the words.*
> *He sounds out letters but can't join them into words e.g. s-a-i-d.*
> *She remembers, does not read what's on the page; she prefers to make up her own story.*

I have a fund of stories aimed at making sense of these enigmas. In answer to the first question above, for example, I explain as follows:

> *When you come again to this room with this group, I shall probably know who you are, but if I meet you in the supermarket on Saturday morning, you will ring a bell in my memory but I shall struggle to put a name to you. I find your face familiar and I'll know you from somewhere but I fail to remember your name. So context affects our ability to remember and it is the same with remembering words on the page. It is easier to read the word 'down' in: 'The rain fell down' than 'Down fell the rain . . .' at the top of a new page where the capital letter is most likely to trigger a name like 'Dawn' appearing in the first place in a sentence . . .*

This way of explaining through metaphor or analogy takes away any hint of parents being dictated to by professionals; parents are free to absorb the point. Our explanatory handout is called *Reading: A Low Key Approach*, and opens in the following way:

> *Have you ever tried to learn to drive with either your wife or your husband? If you are like the majority of us, after a couple of minutes you had a row. The reason is, of course, you bring all your worries and concerns and previous rows and so on into the car with you. This all gets mixed up with your relationship with each other and the stress of the situation. In fact, you are just an argument looking for somewhere to happen!*
>
> *When it comes to teaching your child to read this same danger is there. You obviously are very worried about him; you want him to do well; you are probably also tired yourself and annoyed with some misbehaviour from the previous day; the child may be tired and so on. The reading lesson at home is like the driving lesson — a bomb waiting to explode! On top of all that, the more concerned and caring you are as a parent, the more you are likely to want to give your child more and more practice if he is not making progress. So the reading sessions at home stretch to quarter of an hour, then to half an hour and so on and on. Let's look at this through a child's eyes . . .*

Learning to read is likened to learning to ride a bike: knowing all about bikes – gears chains, handlebars – does not help anyone to ride. You have to risk getting on and actually turning the pedals and steering a course to qualify as a rider. You have to coordinate feet pedalling with arms steering, with eyes looking ahead, judging distances, avoiding obstacles. Reading out loud, too, is a physical skill, requiring the coordination of eye to move along a designated track, ears to listen, fingers to point and tongue to tell the tale. All must follow a rhythm and keep time. Just as with biking, there are wobbles and falls at first, but with successful practice, the movements become automatic. This gives time to enjoy the sensation of competence and to think ahead. To minimise the bad experience of falls and crashes, we run along with the learner until the sequence of movements is flowing. We also provide stabilisers, as we do water wings for swimmers. When you read at the same time as a beginner, you are the stabilisers, ensuring that children keep going without undue failure and achieve the sensation of progress. Once they are confident, they have no need for the support and can set off alone.

So parents appreciate the need to keep the reading going without constant stops and starts to dissect the word-building mechanics. They see that they must not detract from the onward push of the story. Because they are running along with the story, they have only time to keep pace and save breath for praise and comment afterwards. It is no good if the child stops taking responsibility and listens in but omits to keep an eye on the letter by letter route, steering with a finger along the line of print.

Guesses are not random; they are intelligent guesses at what makes sense of the context. Immediate feedback comes with the voice alongside. Never is the learner left in a hole, but can expect help if she meets an unfamiliar word. As long as the pace is controlled by the adult voice sensitive to a workable speed (as is needed in a three-legged race), the child looks, points, scans, listens and speaks, almost at the same instant.

The child benefits from the known rhythms of spoken language and accepted sentence structure. The little words which are so hard to remember in isolation, pass by naturally in context. Looking at pictures and talking about them cannot happen while reading is in progress without risking a hold-up and loss of sense. Aside from the text, pictures can set the scene and predispose the reader to what is likely to happen. Unskilled cyclists wobble because they look at the wheel directly in front and do not have the confidence to look ahead to see where they are going. Once they are practised, they no longer need stabilisers, nor do they have to keep to easy routes. Just as children are proud of their own bikes and like to show off what they can do, so too do children like to choose their own books and demonstrate how well they can read.

In the classroom

Alongside parent practice with paired reading, the eight children met together as a group every morning for six weeks with a teacher (with a remedial reading background). The teacher had years of teaching phonics but with little evidence of transfer of skill to the reading process. All reading was carried out in the simultaneous pattern, whether as a whole group or in pairs with an adult. No story was interrupted to make decoding points. Phonics were taught away from text being read. Children were alerted to rhyme, and to the alphabetic principle in games. Spelling rules were learned in the writing process. The group made up stories orally and produced a joint puppet show for parents at the end of the project as a celebration. They created a written version with the help of a word processor, which allowed easy correction and redrafting. Children copied correct versions so that they were always seeing the right spelling and not habitually practising their own mistakes. Parents with typing skills typed versions of their children's tape-recorded stories or views so that children could scan the correct version while listening to their own voices, matching speech to script as they followed the mapping with their fingers. The motivation for the children to type was high, because they could self-correct without pain, and they were engaged in a public and meaningful activity. They created a book of their own together. Their book bore their names as authors and illustrators, and in practising authorship, they learned meta-cognitive aspects like good beginnings, chapters, surprises of plot and the nature of characters. They thought of exciting adjectives and adverbs. They included rhymes and songs which they adapted. Being able to follow the print because you know the text from memory gave extra practice and confidence. Singing and reciting together with others was also reassuring.

In the short time the children were exposed to many more texts than they would have done by following a scheme. They kept a record of the titles they had tried at home and school, and noted how well they liked their choices. At the beginning they could draw a face, mouth turned up or down to show their mood. It was all right to give up a wrong choice just as adult readers do and to revisit favourites was fine also. They could take books of their choosing home.

To minimise frustration and to promote enjoyment were our goals, and parents testified to the success of these aims. Their children were keen to do reading together and were pushing their parents to sit down with a book. No longer did they feel exposed to failure, but confident that print would yield entertainment. They were excited to talk about the stories and predict outcomes and make up alternative endings. The whole enterprise was no longer fraught and counter-productive. In six weeks many saw themselves as readers and progressed to the independent phase of paired reading. They enjoyed the power of nudging their parents to signal that they wished to go on alone without the helping voice alongside, assured that the voice would re-enter once a difficulty was met on the track. Parents, too, were no longer seeking refuge in labels like dyslexia or scapegoating teachers to explain failure, but were feeling themselves to be the agents of change.

A rationale for the success witnessed

I propose that the combination of key factors below contributed to the successes seen in this venture:

- A relaxed environment and reduced anxiety
- Failure-free practice
- Focus on strengths not weaknesses
- Close home–school liaison
- Empowerment of parents and children and increased confidence
- Emphasis on the motivation of choice of book and reading for pleasure
- Learning to read implicitly by reading (not coming explicitly 'to learn to read')
- Increased exposure to text
- Holistic, multi-sensory approaches
- Placing search for shared meaning in central position
- Recognition of the importance of talking about stories
- Recognition of the importance of talking about text, i.e. meta-cognitive aspects
- Use of the group dynamic and collaborative learning
- Use of games, puppets, songs, rhymes

and

- Decoding skills taught *separately* from actual reading sessions through games
- Spelling learned in the writing process, by practice of *encoding* skills.

Any of these features could be the focus of investigation, but I judge it is the whole combination that is significant. A social context of learning alongside friends and family has been created and the scene has been freed from blame and anxiety. Within a supportive climate, skills have been practised without the disruptive emotions of panic. Writing and reading are joined as complementary activities, conducted for a real social purpose. Within this safe haven, it so happens that phonemic awareness is developed. Thus, an apprenticeship model is allied to the findings of research which have been used to discredit such meaning-making models. Just how this alliance works in practice is the subject of the remaining part of this chapter.

Increased exposure to text

Much of the contention about reading approaches centres on the nature of the exposure to text given. It is sometimes said that real book exponents throw children into a sea of wonderful books without water wings or armbands to keep them afloat. Of course, left alone without any mediation, a child will flounder (Dombey 1993). Paired reading allows much exposure before the child is an independent decoder, and the supporting voice means s/he does not flounder in frustration. Meaningless tasks are what are frustrating. So, reading along in a relaxed manner with adult support allows failure-free reading, and access to the story line. It therefore breeds the desire to read more and more. Choosing books and assuming ownership of the reading session are empowering for the children, who are then disposed to pay attention and find out what the print represents. They gain the advantages of fluency before they have accuracy. The fact that they are following their co-readers a fraction of a second behind them does not mean they are cheating and that the whole affair is a hoax or that it condemns the child to be for ever yoked to a mentor.

While copying, they are in fact learning the valuable knowledge that sounds of speech are represented on the page in the left to right pattern. This scanning and linking of sound and print is the correct procedure and not a habit that has to be unlearned. If children are kept away from books that exceed their decoding skill, they are confined to a small selection of specially designed books and these are not readily available to ordinary parents, who are excluded from reading what a child chooses and what is easily to hand.

McGuinness encourages parents to read to their children and to enjoy nursery rhymes, but to regard teaching of reading as an expert skill of imparting the alphabetic code to learners in a prescribed order. She claims that many of her 'clients' do not realise that print is a code at all, and in their ignorance, they resort to harmful strategies, which let them down. I too have come across children who rely exclusively on memory or who recite letter names or who misuse phonic training, and there is no one culprit. Paired reading, however, cannot be culpable; the child who traces the print while hearing and saying the words must surely come to realise that a representational code is involved. Unlocking the actual code is another matter and the central question is how much is learned implicitly and how much is learned explicitly.

Implicit and explicit learning

At SPRInt, the children were exposed to the link between sounds and letters implicitly while reading along. They were also shown explicit links in games apart from the reading process itself, and in the context of writing.

We all agree that unlearning something is wasteful and difficult. Therefore, ensuring that the right messages are conveyed from the start would be ideal. I find that parents are saved from being teachers when they pair-read and this prevents pointless sounding out of every letter (as with s-a-i-d), and other garbled applications of phonics. They simply give the right word and the right spelling without any discussion.

McGuinness has highlighted the dangers of mistaken phonics programmes. She decries the fact that phonics programmes teach the alphabetic principle 'backwards': they teach that 'letters have sounds' rather than that 'speech' has sounds and these speech sounds 'have letters'. 'Traditional phonics teaches the sounds of letters. The other way, which doesn't yet have a name, teaches the sound (phonemes) in the English language and how each of these phonemes are mapped to letters' (McGuinness 1988: 101).

She is very precise in how to make this mapping explicit to learners:

> Children learn that a letter is a 'picture' for one sound. This makes it clear what is being symbolised. Just as real objects can be drawn in pictures, so can real sounds be drawn as pictures. This terminology helps later when the child is introduced to sound-pictures that have more than one letter. The teacher should say something like: 'Words are made up of sounds. Letters are sound pictures for each of these sounds. It's like when you draw a picture of a dog or a house. This is the sound picture (b) for the sound /b/ in the "bat".' Show the child the letter or point to it. Do not use letter names. (ibid.: 232)

I believe that this mapping is conveyed while reading along, and provides the basis for understanding that 'sounds have letters'. Whereas McGuinness overcomes the problem that in English, there are 'too many sounds chasing too few letters', by systematically teaching the most likely spellings first and has constructed tables arranged according to spelling probabilities to guide this process, I put forward the proposition that reading a wide range of books means that children are exposed to the probabilities in a naturally occurring situation. Frequently seeing and hearing words as they are read helps children make inferences about the links between sounds and letters.

Making cross-modal connections

Reading along ensures that the *eye* sees the script as the *voice* speaks the words and the *finger* traces the sequence. This almost simultaneous tying of sensory modes is powerful. Feedback is also instantaneous without being disconcerting. The supporting partner allows the learner to get the feel of the activity before s/he is at the stage of automaticity and the sensory-motor organisation occurs as a result of the experience.

On SPRInt, the children also became aware of the sound-spelling links in the *encoding* rather than the *decoding* situation: they had to convert speech into script to write their stories. The first stage was to dictate their ideas to a scribe to ensure a correct version to read together. Also, easy spelling rules were learned in games and this knowledge informed the reading and writing process.

Collaborative learning

McGuinness rules out group learning categorically (1988: 318). She cites the embarrassment of being shown up and the differing rates of acquiring the necessary logic as thorns in the group approach. By contrast, I know the group dynamic can be used as a positive incentive. Working with a facilitator-teacher, the children need not see others as rivals and competitors, but as collaborators in a joint enterprise. The skills of a good drawer or puppet-maker can be recognised as useful to the whole endeavour, and children can ask each other for help, compose together and negotiate about what to include. The focus of attention is not on the business of reading, but on creating and composing and making of puppets and props for dramatisation. Strengths are more salient than mistakes or weaknesses. Singing and reciting poems together as well as producing a play all foster group cohesion.

Motivation is high when children want to record something of personal or of group importance. When writing makes human sense, because it is a real communication with significant others, re-drafting and copying a fair version are not a dreary exercise but a purposeful task. The children were not pursuing a long-term goal imposed by adults who know the value of literacy, but undertaking a joint endeavour which would have a public airing very soon, when the parents came for the puppet show.

Place of parents

Parents were essential to the success of this project. Buoyed up by understanding the rationale and having clear procedures, they relaxed with their children and enjoyed sharing stories without former anxiety. McGuinness devotes a whole chapter to extolling the importance of parents and recognising how they share in the pain of reading failure. She notes that 'parents' emotions are sometimes even more important than the child's in producing a successful outcome' (1988: 299). For her, their main value is in their commitment to 'delivering their child to the reading specialist', who can give one-to-one attention in remedying false strategies by applying the Phono-Graphix approach. They can pay out money for services, and fight for their children to have specialist help. If they decide they can teach themselves, they are directed to the method outlined for conveying the alphabetic principle. They are led to believe that since most teachers are misinformed about this principle, there is little hope within the school system. The book's doom-laden viewpoint about declining standards of literacy in English-speaking countries adds to the culture of blame on educators. Fuelling distrust and anxiety can only be detrimental; more important is enabling relationships of mutual respect between parents and teachers.

There are renewed opportunities for small groups to author books with a facilitating adult, even within the Literacy Hour framework. Constructing texts together with a mediating adult channelling children's interests can once again find a place. Joint working between home and school can ensure that children come to reading predisposed to like it and to make sense of it.

Conversation with Nigel Mellor, author of *Cuddle and Read*, a guide for parents

I asked Nigel how *Cuddle and Read* came about. Nigel explained that it was created in response to the finding that, out of frustration, irritation and anxiety, many parents resorted to confrontational and negative reading sessions with their failing children. One parent confessed to hitting her child over the head with a newspaper every time he made a mistake. His booklet shows how reading together can become a pleasant experience once again. Once parents see learning to read as the same as learning a skill, like riding a bike, they handle the session more sensitively. They see that the child is not being deliberately awkward or inattentive: s/he is simply struggling with a skill that has yet to become automatic. Uncertainty and error are normal parts of the process.

He said that what happens in these home-reading sessions is a 'largely overlooked issue' (Greenhough and Hughes 1998: 384). It might be instructive to look at the physiological research, which has shown connections between visual and limbic pathways in the brain, highlighting the role of emotion in perception (as outlined in Challoner 2000). Most research has instead concentrated on seeking correlations between certain supposed components of the reading process – like visual discrimination or auditory memory – and the successful reader. The power of the 'psychological processes model' lies in 'some kind of face validity', and the ease with which measurement can yield results. Once some positive correlations emerge, we seek to train children in these presumed sub-skills. A 'myth' about the significance of these components builds up, and 'people trot out remedial schemes and teaching schedules as if they are the pearls of wisdom and the tablets of truth'. Any contrary research which then shows 'massive holes in the underlying assumptions' is then ignored (e.g. Hamill and Larsen 1974).

Perhaps a more fruitful route would be to emphasise the impact of stress and anxiety on perception and consequently on performance. We all know we cannot see something right under our noses when we are searching in hasty agitation. Furthermore, perception itself is a matter of confidence, as is borne out by signal detection theory. If we are intent on discovering enemy planes on a radar screen, we are likely to firm up a faint and ambiguous signal into a certainty, because the consequences of discounting it would be dangerous. In contrast, the feeling that you might have seen a ghost is dismissed for fear of being regarded as a fool. So, perceptions are not simple either/or (yes/no) experiences, but often the 'best guess in the circumstances'.

Nigel: It's guessing about faint, confusing, ambiguous signals, hidden in a mess of other confusing and ambiguous signals. How you feel at that time, and how stressed you are, will determine whether you see it or whether you don't see it. It's not an either/or. It's how you feel about it. Obviously some things you do see and that's sort of clear, but when it's in this marginal area of uncertainty . . . The trouble is that we look upon hearing and seeing as simple processes like taking a picture and that's as far as we get. But it's much more subtle and sophisticated than that:

emotions come into it; your confidence in seeing something comes into it, particularly in ambiguous situations; your constructs come into it; what you think you're going to see. We create what we're going to see, so perceptions are a construction.

Because our general understanding of hearing and seeing is so much rooted in a very old-fashioned model, a very simplistic model, we can't see any other way to think about seeing.

Fleur: I think that's the case with the new-born infant: it actually turns to look at what it hears. The two systems are inextricably bound and yet in our thinking we see it as a visual process or a hearing process. Likewise, we see reading as if it's this channel or that channel when they're not separate channels; they're totally linked from the beginning of development and therefore you've got to do a reading process that is amalgamated. You get on the bike and ride!

Nigel: That's right, yes.

Fleur: We can't do a bit of reading that's to do with visual and a bit of something that is to do with hearing and hope that it somehow integrated.

Nigel: You can't learn pedalling on a bench and learn steering on a bench and learn balance on a bench.

Fleur: Yes, and then hope it goes together.

Nigel: And then hope it will all go together.

Fleur: And the same thing applies, I think, to learning of language, that when children with language deficits are then taught bits of language, like how to do the pronouns or how to do prepositions.

Nigel: Yes; in, on and under!

Fleur: In, on and under. It's actually the same story; it then doesn't add together like a communication.

We finished by talking specifically of children with speech and language difficulties, who often become the subjects of remedial reading initiatives. Just as we try and create situations which prompt functional communication, so we also bring some agency (and urgency) into the reading process.

Fleur: With many of these children with speech and language difficulties, it's going to be too big a gap between their language facility and the language of the books. But, they do really like literacy in terms of agency: they love being able to turn the flaps, open the windows and so we use a lot of those kind of books to start with, because if you can't take on the language, you can actually take on the point to the story. Something opens, something closes, something jumps out.

Nigel: That's right, yes.

Fleur: Something pops out and you can enjoy the emotional sense of an unfolding plot even though you're not necessarily taking part in the language. If you don't do that, what happens is that you start getting taught how to put the c- a- t together and that then ends up as what you do for years. I can think of a child who ended up at twelve, still doing c- a- t. So the phonics hasn't helped him at all and he can never move on because he hasn't got past the c- v- c stage.

Nigel pointed out that here was a child, for whom the 'bottom-up' model had not taken him from the building blocks up to the building's roof, from sub-skills to sense. Instead he has gone from 'phonics to nonsense', and never gets to the sense of it all. Others enjoy the journey up, but without seeing the view from the top.

Nigel: I think in a funny way some children might benefit from these interventions which draw them into parts of the process, simply because they're getting a bit of success. The programmes are in very small steps and they love repetition, clear goals. So for once in their lives, the kids are getting some success with something resembling bits of reading, so they think they're making progress, so their confidence builds up. As a kind of spin-off, their reading might improve, simply because they're feeling better about themselves and again getting a bit of success for once.

Fleur: I think that's part of the reason why paired reading works. When parents read along with their children a lot, people could say the same thing: at last, children are getting some attention, some success.

Nigel: And also it takes the heat out of the situation. It takes the social pressure off the children.

Everyone can keep calm and pay joint attention to understanding a chosen story in a cuddle-up context.

CHAPTER 9

Social Interactionism in Practice: A Review

Marion Farmer

The aim of this chapter is to demonstrate the support given by theory and research for the use of a child-centred, naturalistic, conversational approach in assessment and intervention with children with communication delays and difficulties. A description of the principles and premises of the theoretical base which supports these ideas will be advanced first, followed by a review of practice and research based on this approach.

Theoretical models of the normal development of language and communication skills are the basis for our current array of assessment devices and methods in this area. They are also the basis for the aims and methods of intervention programmes with children whose development of these skills is in some way considered to be impaired. These theoretical perspectives vary in the role that they have played in the development of assessment methods and in their usefulness in the development of intervention methods. In the main, as argued below, approaches that address not only the description of the communicative skills of the child at different ages, but also the *process* by which skills are developed and learned, have been the most useful, since they provide the practitioner not only with targets for intervention but also with a theoretical basis from which to develop the intervention methods themselves.

Nelson (1993) provides a helpful summary of the main theoretical positions on language development and classifies them into six main types:

1 Biological maturation theories which tie language acquisition to the innate maturational processes of brain structures (Marshall 1981).
2 Linguistic rule induction theories which are in fact a sub-set of biological maturation theories in that they propose that we have an innate language acquisition device that is biologically based and only triggered by the environment (e.g. Chomsky 1965, 1981; Pinker 1987).
3 Behaviourism which focuses on the observable and measurable aspects of language behaviour and the mechanisms by which children learn to produce these 'functional units' of verbal behaviour (Skinner 1957).
4 Cognitivist theories (the prime example being the all-encompassing theory of Piaget, e.g. Piaget 1926) which suggest that language development is a sub-set of cognitive

development and therefore depends on and is shaped by the development of general cognitive structures.

5 Information-processing theories, a sub-set of cognitivist theories, which are concerned with the processes underpinning cognitive acts and are concerned with the way linguistic stimuli are encoded, represented, manipulated, stored and retrieved (Johnson-Laird 1983).

6 Social interaction theories which suggest that language is a socio-cultural tool which develops out of social encounters as a consequence of human motivation to interact with others and to develop a concept of self (Vygotsky 1962; Bruner 1968). It is the latter theories with which this book is principally concerned since, as I will contend, they provide a basis for blending content and procedures into a unified assessment and intervention approach with young children. For an extended discussion of the usefulness of the various types of theory see Nelson (1993).

Social interaction theory suggests that children learn to talk and practise their communication skills when they have a reason to do so, and that context determines the language structures that are used. Nelson (1993) summarises the primary assumptions of social interactionist theories of language development as follows:

1 Language develops not because of any innate linguistic competence or because of strict reinforcement principles, but because human beings are motivated to interact socially and to develop concepts of self and others.

2 The important elements of development are not abstract linguistic or cognitive structures or concrete verbal behaviours, but rather they are the phenomena of intentional and symbolic acts of speech, their conversational functions, their consequences for participants and their context-creating power and context-dependent properties.

3 Language acquisition occurs in the content of dyadic, dynamic interactions which are motivated by the child's drive to develop a concept of self and to interact with others socially (not isolated efforts to construct a grammar, or passive processes controlled by external reinforcers).

4 Parents (and other conversational partners) contribute significantly to the language acquisition process by adjusting their linguistic input to be compatible with the child's developing linguistic and communicative abilities and by supplying a scaffold.

The important distinction between this approach and others outlined above is that it focuses on *the processes* by which communication and language develop. It is not so much concerned with the 'what' of development, but with the 'how'. Of the other types of theory described above only behaviourism is concerned with the detail of the learning process and in fact, as Nelson (1993) says, 'offers a technology for designing procedural approaches to language assessment and intervention that is more developed than that provided by any other theoretical perspective'. One of the main problems with behaviourism is that it ignores meaning and intention. If we break language behaviour into small targets to be produced as response units, then meaning and intention are lost and the units that the child is taught do not readily generalise to communication in the everyday world. For social interactionists, on the other hand, the development of shared meaning and shared understanding in relationships is central rather than peripheral, as is the sensitive scaffolding of interactive encounters by which this is achieved. This theoretical base provides us with a rationale for dissecting the relationship between more competent and less competent communicative partners, and relating our analyses of interpersonal processes to developmental achievements. Context is also considered to be an essential part of the meaning. Therefore the problems of generalisation inherent in other approaches should not exist. The rationale for its use in therapeutic and other relationships is that optimum, natural development appears to be achieved in this way (see evidence below).

A concept, employed by the theory, which should be elaborated here since it is of particular importance to those who adopt the social interactionist model in therapeutic and educational settings, is that of the Zone of Proximal Development (ZPD). This is described as 'the difference between a child's actual developmental level as determined by independent problem-solving and the level of potential development as determined through problem-solving under adult guidance or in collaboration with more capable peers' (Vygotsky 1978). Thus Schneider and Watkins (1996), who advocate the use of Vygotskian ideas as the basis for assessment and intervention, suggest that when children are working with an adult or more competent partner they are able to operate at a higher level of competence than when they are operating alone, if the adult structures the activity in a way that is sensitive to each child's current level and needs. To do this they suggest *intersubjectivity* must be established, i.e. the two must establish an agreed definition of the situation, a shared understanding of the meaning of the situation. In order for this to happen, the adult must attempt to understand the child's situation-definition and negotiate from there to a definition which is acceptable to both. At the earlier stages of development it is the child's attention which the adult must negotiate to gain, later it is the nature of the activity to be undertaken. Thus if they are confronted with a set of building blocks which the child wishes to throw and the adult wishes to use for construction it is up to the adult to negotiate a definition which the child accepts and which is closer to the adult's own definition. The adult carries on these negotiations through *semiotic mediation* or adaptation of their assistance (*scaffolding*) to help the child participate in the activity. Adults adjust this assistance from moment to moment in the interaction and gradually give more responsibility to the child – leading to *abbreviated assistance* on the part of the adult. The adult switches between abbreviated and unabbreviated help, sensitive to the child's needs. The children are learning not only how to complete particular activities but also how to identify the steps involved in completing an activity. Schaffer also says the adult's role is not to create new cognitive processes but to facilitate, direct and extend those that have already appeared. He suggests that there is

> increasing evidence that social interactive experiences affect cognitive growth and that their influence in the early years is most effectively transmitted in the context

of . . . joint involvement episodes . . . that entail the mutual co-operation of a participant child and a sensitive adult. (1996: 239).

Evidence to support this can be found in research such as that of Pratt *et al.* (1988), Garton (1992) and Barbieri and Landolfi (1994).

The premises of social interactionist theory are validated by much evidence from investigations of children's communicative development. Thus research with normally developing children has used both observational and experimental methods to investigate whether aspects of the environment and aspects of communicative interchanges advocated by this theoretical stance promote greater communicative competence in children. Therefore, for instance, it has been found that child-centred exchanges in social interaction, where the mother or more mature partner follows the child's focus of attention and provides language to accompany that focus, predicts later size of vocabulary (e.g. Tomasello and Farrar 1986; Harris 1992). It has also been shown that conversational recast strategies where the mother repeats the child's utterance with expansion promote the acquisition of syntactical structures (Nelson 1977; Baker and Nelson 1984; Scherer and Olswang 1984). Hart (2000) summarises a great deal of this evidence and also her own findings based on extended observational studies of children learning to talk within the home, and intervention studies with children struggling to develop their communication skills, by saying that research reveals how crucial to development is the amount of children's language experience as partners in the 'social dances of conversation'. She identifies adult attention, partnerships and amount of language exposure as the keys to the enhancement of communication skills. She suggests that the reciprocal nature of the partnership is the key and that in mother–child communication real reciprocal partnerships occur in low-demand situations where only social consequences are on offer, where what each partner says is governed by what the other said. Each partner has to listen, maintain the topic and elaborate in order to keep the conversation going. In her research, differences between parents were observed in how much they talked to their children, their responsiveness to children's chosen topics, their guidance to the child through questions rather than commands and the variety of their talk about things and relationships. These differences were reflected in the communicative development of their children. Hart, however, also suggests that we still need to investigate these parameters further in order to understand the nature of the partnerships between parents and children and to evaluate the frequency with which children, especially children with language delays, are acting as partners rather than turn-takers during interactions. Warren (2000) similarly summarised the ideal responsive conditions for the enhancement of the development of language and communication skills in children. By responsive he means a style of dyadic interaction in which a child regularly experiences a wide range of natural teaching devices such as expansions; models; growth recasts; use of concrete, simplified vocabulary; talk about objects and events to which the child is attending; all finely tuned to the child's comprehension level. He asserts that 'this style of interaction appears to aid the acquisition of linguistic and communicative competence in most children (Gallaway and Richards 1994) and may be even more important for children with developmental disorders and delays (Yoder *et al.* 1998).

Applying theory to practice

The focus of this book is on assessment and intervention with children with communication difficulties and the application of theory to investigations in this area. So first of all, assessment – what is assessment? What is its purpose? As Pellegrini (2001) suggests, 'assessment refers to the process of collecting information on children . . . in order to make inferences about their status'. Two main types are evident: 'high stakes' assessment on which placement and resources decisions will depend and which will provide the background for intervention; and intervention-focused assessment, designed to inform the teaching and learning relationships and methods to be adopted with the child.

Second, intervention – what is intervention? What is its purpose? The answer appears to lie in our social construction of individual identity. In our society, we purport to value each human life and to consider that it is important that each should not only survive, but also should fulfil their potential as an individual. We perceive individuals as intrinsically social and as unable to survive without a social context. We also see the necessity for individuals to conform to the demands of their social context by abiding by social rules, values and mores and valuing and respecting the needs of others. We wish to enable developing individuals to overcome obstacles to integration into the social world, to function 'appropriately' within whatever cultural context may be present. Therefore, with individuals perceived as in some way lacking in the abilities to fit in, to conform, to cope with survival, to fulfil their potential, we set up interventions to enable them to develop the appropriate abilities and competencies to achieve these aims. These interventions are, of course, shaped by the cultural context in which the individual is found. Within the cultural context in which we write, the means for achieving goals are variously shaped by the medical and scientific and educational background to our thinking.

Within the medical framework and scientific framework we feel the need to identify logically the precise nature of the abilities/disabilities of individuals in order to understand the nature of what we perceive to be their social misfit and in order to focus our interventions precisely. So we theorise, we build our models, we test them, we attempt to evaluate their effectiveness in predicting behaviours and outcomes and we hope that we come ever closer to an understanding of the complexities of the interleaved, and indeed inextricably intertwined, layers of the human neurological, emotional, cognitive, psychological and social self.

As a result of these very complexities, however, a variety of models have been developed that often only focus on one level of the developing self and tend to ignore the others. In science, this can be seen as helpful in isolating the minutiae of mechanisms that underlie complex functions. However, when the science is applied to intervention with the individual, the individual is inevitably functioning during the intervention at the most complex level, the social, subsuming all other layers of the self. What seems to happen with many assessments and interventions is that this fact is ignored. We attempt to identify deficits in the child's performance which we theorise are caused by some underlying deficiency in processing, rule-making or representation, but this identification, based on a static model of the language system, does not entail an under-standing of the processes of development and change which are responsible for the child's functional competence. It is indeed at this level, the level of change and development, that we need our theories to be most efficient and perceptive.

Within the educational framework, by contrast, the focus is on the processes of development and learning and the methods for enabling all individuals to reach their potential academically, socially and personally. The aim therefore is to look at the nature of the child's learning processes and environments that promote that learning rather than to identify hypothetical deficits in the child's make-up. As a result, the careful identification of the perceptual underpinnings of a child's performance tends to be ignored. 'Deficit' analysis is seen as a labelling and categorising process which has led to doubtful practices of categorisation and exclusion. There is a mismatch here in approaches which dogs the literature and bedevils research attempts.

There is a divorce between needs of different disciplines. Cognitive neuroscience, medicine and other disciplines require categories and clear definitions in order to under-stand human acts of cognition. Education requires an understanding of the processes of development and learning. Is it possible to reconcile these approaches? Can we use information obtained about the child's 'deficits' to inform our understanding of the learning processes taking place? Can categorical deficit models be reframed to continua of strengths and weaknesses of function and the effects of learning and environments? In theory, this should be possible, but much of the literature in the past has focused on the identification of deficits without the complementary application of the informa-tion to learning so that many educationists are unhappy with the labelling and diagnos-ing that accompany assessment as we know it and find it unhelpful in the extreme (for a discussion of labelling see Riddick 2000). Education needs functional, valid and viable methods of assessment and intervention. These methods should take into account indi-vidual differences and variability, but should not look for rigidly defined 'treatments' for the developmental deficits and disorders. They should also accommodate the wide range of issues in relating to children and their families. This is where social interaction-ist approaches have much to offer. Vygotskian ideas focus on the social processes which facilitate learning and are therefore highly applicable to the educational agenda.

Assessment methods and practice

As defined above, assessment involves the collecting of information. Good assessment is very important and useful in providing information but a major problem is children's lack of motivation to perform in a situation that is uninteresting and anxiety-producing. Social interactionist theory suggests that natural activities provide us with the best infor-mation about functional competence. Given this, many practitioners attempting to adopt these ideas advocate play as the arena for assessment with young children since play is 'what children do when they are not involved in activities that meet biological needs or that are required by adults' (Singer 1973). Here we can find children using their skills for the purpose of their own entertainment, relaxed or making an effort as they wish, messing about, following obsessions, concentrating, exploring communicating if they wish. Generally most practitioners would recommend observations of the child's natural play behaviour as part at least of the process of assessment. Many practitioners also recommend additional more structured scenarios. Of course the approach advocated depends at least in part on the function of the assessment. Is it 'high stakes' assessment on which placement and resources decisions will depend or is it intervention-focused, designed to inform the teaching and learning relationships and methods to be adopted with the child?

Pellegrini (2001) provides a most useful comprehensive advocacy for the observation of play in the assessment of young children. He suggests that it is very important that 'all assessment should make very explicit what it is assessing, if for no other reason than the fact that assessment has an impact on the lives of children, their families and schools'. He summarises the reasons why the assessment of young children by means of tests is an unreliable business as follows:

1 Test–retest reliability coefficients are typically low because children's performance varies considerably, depending upon a number of ecological features: familiarity with the context; familiarity with the props; familiarity with the assessor; race and sex of the assessor, other anxiety related to teacher, parent or self.
2 Tests assess a very limited universe of competence, being concerned primarily with low-level cognitive processes and not with the social and emotional aspects of their development.

Pellegrini goes on to describe the relevance of the play situation for assessment, basing many of his ideas on the Vygotskian concept of play. He explains that for Vygotsky play created a 'zone of proximal development in which children exhibit higher levels of competence than when outside the zone'. The play context itself acts in the way that a more competent partner might to allow the child to operate at their optimum levels of competence. 'In play there is a wonderful mixture of children being motivated and this motivation is directed towards highly sophisticated goals; this allows them to exhibit higher levels of competence in play than in more traditional assessment contexts.' Pellegrini suggests that therefore 'play seems like an almost "too good to be true" answer to the problem of assessing young children'.

The type of play advocated in this instance does not include solitary play, but uses what Pellegrini calls 'the paradigm case of play' for pre-school children (defined here as ages 3 to 6 years): 'social pretend'. The basic criteria which Pellegrini takes for play are the following: it should be purposeless, i.e. the activity is more important than the outcome; and it should be accompanied by positive affect. Pellegrini suggests that 'a particularly fruitful approach to assessing young children involves observing them as they interact with their peers in situations which are simultaneously motivating and demanding of high levels of social cognitive processing'. Pellegrini also notes that children exhibit higher levels of social, cognitive and linguistic skills when they are assessed with a friend, compared to an acquaintance. Social role play demands perspective-taking and the communication of fantasy which demands sophisticated oral language. Pellegrini and Galda (1998) suggest that children's use of language in social fantasy play is a reliable predictor of later literacy development in primary school. Pellegrini offers two observation schedules for use in the observation of children at play and also much advice on procedures to be followed in order that observations should be valid.

Many other practitioners also offer suggestions for the use of play as the basis of assessment of children's communicative, social and cognitive abilities. A well-researched example of this for use in 'high stakes' assessment with children who present as possibly on the autistic spectrum is ADOS, the Autism Direct Observation Schedule. This is a play-based standardised protocol which presents the child with a series of structured and semi-structured situations for observing interaction, communication, repetitive behaviours and play. Specific behaviours as well as general ratings of the child's social-communicative function are coded (Lord *et al.* 1989).

Another example which has less specific focus and aims to inform intervention is Linder's Trans-disciplinary Play-Based Assessment and Intervention (1993). This is a functional assessment process designed for children between the ages of six months and six years and examines a child's performance across all areas of development (including social and communicative) while s/he interacts with a play facilitator who follows the child's lead; with parents or caregivers; a peer or group of peers. It revolves around assessments by observation by a multi-disciplinary team and takes around one hour to an hour and a half. The process can take place in any environment with which the child is familiar such as a pre-school classroom or the child's home, as long as an appropriate range of toys is available. As described by the author, this assessment follows the move away from assessment of isolated skills and the use of tests that result in numbers and labels but no practical suggestions. She suggests that 'the search for functional practical assessment approaches has resulted in a shift to assessing children in less restricted functional settings involving collaborative efforts of professionals and families'. This assessment is usefully matched with linked naturalistic intervention approaches as recommended in a companion manual.

A further approach to assessment which is based on social interactionist principles, but is not necessarily linked to the use of play is that advocated by Schneider and Watkins (1996). They discuss the use of *dynamic assessment* based on key ideas from Vygotsky's developmental theory and its applications to assessment and to intervention with children with language impairments. Schneider and Watkins remind us that Vygotsky originally introduced the notion of the ZPD (zone of proximal development) as a means of assessing children's potential for learning as an alternative to the static measures of IQ and mental age. ZPD has been incorporated into *dynamic assessment* which is used to assess the process of a child's learning – rather than the product of learning which is assessed by standard assessment techniques such as standardised tests. Schneider and Watkins suggest that in language assessment dynamic assessment can be used to assess a child's responsiveness to different types of therapy and thus to decide on the most appropriate intervention for that child. They actually suggest that the child who is less responsive to therapy is the one who requires intervention since the more responsive child will probably achieve the relevant target through maturation without the need for much intervention. In their paper Schneider and Watkins also distinguish between the *quantitative* and *qualitative* goals of dynamic assessment. The quantitative goal aims to inform decisions about whether a child is a suitable candidate for intervention in relation to a pre-determined goal at a particular point in time. The question to be answered is: how modifiable is the child? How much will a child benefit by a programme of interventions?) The qualitative goal aims to identify the skills a child is currently developing but cannot evidence independently, i.e. in which contexts and with what types of assistance a child can perform an activity. The question to be answered is: For which skills and at which levels is adult assistance helpful?) Much of the work in dynamic assessment has focused on children's modifiability, but Schneider and Watkins, however, are concerned with the qualitative approach, focusing on what goes on in dynamic interaction and how the adult adjusts assistance to mediate for the child in particular points in the interaction. Schneider and Watkins illustrate their arguments with the presentation of a number of instances of the use of dynamic assessment in language assessment.

This approach seems to embody all the tenets of the social interactionist approach but also to present real challenges in terms of time and training for practitioners. However, the integration of assessment with intervention as part of an ongoing process has much to recommend it in the economy of the approach and the validity of activities for both child and family.

Research into intervention

If we now turn to intervention, we can see that there is some concern evident in the research literature over the models of intervention currently used and the effectiveness of speech therapy in practice. Thus Glogowska *et al.* (2000) attempted to assess the long-term effectiveness of speech and language therapy for pre-school children with appreciable speech and language difficulties. Children were randomly assigned to a therapy group or a control group where no therapy but 'watchful waiting' ensued. They were assessed on a variety of measures both standardised and observational including assessments of language, phonological skills, daily living, socialisation and motor skills, attention, symbolic play and parent perceptions at 6 and 12 months from their baseline assessment. Children assigned to the therapy group received one-to-one speech therapy routinely offered by the therapist. The results of their study showed that there was little evidence for the effectiveness of speech and language therapy compared with 'watchful waiting' over 12 months. They suggest that further research into more specific types of provision with sub-groups of children is required to identify better treatment methods.

Responses to Glogowska *et al.*, however, do suggest that this study highlights the inadequacy of the amount of speech and language therapy offered routinely to children rather than the ineffectiveness of therapy in itself. These children received only 6 hours of therapy in a 12-month period. Law and Conti-Ramsden (2000) point out that previous studies have shown significant positive effects of speech therapy when less limited amounts are offered and a more flexible approach is taken to the needs of each child in the choice of intervention package. Certainly there is room for consideration here of exactly how resources are allocated and what interventions are advocated. However, we must acknowledge that access to the resources of skilled personnel will always be limited and therefore rather than providing one-to-one clinic-based services, intervening to facilitate more sensitive and supportive interactions between parents and children should be considered as an important way forward, on both theoretical and pragmatic grounds.

The argument against this, of course, is that these children have been receiving 'naturalistic' input from their parents up to the date of professional involvement and have failed to make progress. Surely more of the same is not the answer. However, if we turn to studies of the interaction between mothers and children with SLI we find that these show that the conversations of mothers with these children are different from those with normally developing children. For example, several studies have found that mothers (or other carers) are more directive in their speech and provide fewer conversational recasts to these children than to normally developing children at similar levels of language development (Conti-Ramsden and Dykins 1991; Nelson et al. 1996). Similarly with autistic children who do not seek communication, it has been found that their interactional difficulties tend to make parents adopt an intrusive interactional style with their children. Thus adults attempt to encourage communication from their children by directing and questioning – which leads to a breakdown in the sharing of meaning (Shapiro et al. 1987). Since interaction with parents is the main arena in which communication is developed, it seems important, from the social interactionist viewpoint, that this is where intervention should start.

An interesting, but quite unusually radical, example of this is provided by Ward (1999), who describes a language intervention based on natural principles and research with very young children identified as communication delayed in the first year of life. In a programme based on the social interactionist approach, parents were taught to modify their interactions with these children to provide the infants with sufficient input of the appropriate quality in an environment in which they were able to benefit from this. Interventions were done in the children's own homes and tailored to the children's individual needs. No expressive output was required during the interventions – it was entirely based on giving appropriate input. No attachment of deficit labels was included. The intervention was presented as a facilitation of normal development. Following the intervention it was found that all but three of the children who completed the intervention were within normal language development limits at three years, compared to only 15 per cent of matched controls. Ward concluded that there is a sensitive period where relatively small amounts of finely tuned appropriate intervention are effective.

Ward's early and very general approach seems to have much to offer, if such an approach could be widely available. However, even if this were the case, it would not be possible to implement it in all situations (selective parent non-participation and identification errors are bound to occur) and, as noted above, some children presented with difficulties despite this approach. The clear identification of communication difficulties does not usually take place until at least the age of two years since there is wide variability within the normally developing population in the ages of attainment of developmental milestones. By this time the normal parent–child partnership in communication is likely to have developed a dysfunctional pattern.

There are now a number of social interactionist approaches to intervention with young children who have been clearly identified as having specific difficulties in the development of communication. These approaches seek to build on the social interactionist model of the development of communication and language, and use its premises to build up communicative intent, social responsiveness and language skills in children with communicative difficulties, such as autism and other pervasive developmental disorders and children with language impairments and delays. Examples of these are the Child's Talk project (Aldred *et al.* 2001), Smith and Fluck's (2000) social interactional games programme and the Hanen programme (Manolson 1992).

Thus the Child's Talk programme has been designed for 'children with core autism and autistic spectrum disorder at either the pre-verbal or early stages of language development'. Intervention starts in the home environment but is equally applicable to all educational and social environments. Both parents are involved and their individual styles observed and adapted to achieve an equivalent understanding of the underlying principles involved in developing social communication. Early intervention is aimed at repairing the breakdown in early social exchange on which it is premised later communication skills are based. So Child's Talk focuses on establishing social engagement and joint attention in natural interactions. The central theme is to promote synchrony in carer–child interactions. The outcomes of a study of the use of this programme with 40 children with autism and their families are not yet available but should provide interesting evidence as to the efficacy of the approach and the pitfalls of implementation and evaluation.

Another intervention programme utilising social interactionist principles, reported by Smith and Fluck (2000) and now available commercially (Smith and Fluck 2001) is not specifically aimed at children with autism. The reported research study implementing the programme addressed the difficulties of a mixed group of children aged 3–5 years with limited communication skills. None of the children had passed beyond the stage of producing one-word utterances and many were silent, or produced only a few sounds. Baseline observations had indicated that the usual pattern of mutual attention and interpersonal shared imitation was either delayed or distorted. The theoretical underpinnings of the programme are those of Vygotsky and Bruner, and the basic premise is that 'a major part of the framework within which the linguistic and non-linguistic components of conversation are acquired may be the pragmatic context provided by shared games'. A graded series of social games formats forms the basis for the intervention. Basically the social games formats involved nursery staff and parents in choosing specific game formats for the children in order to foster social non-verbal and verbal communication. The adult's activity is child-centred in that the adult starts by playing alongside the child in non-interactive and silent ways in a deliberately constructed context of joint space. Child and adult have similar materials. The adult then uses exact copies of the child's objects and imitates the actions of the child. Simple labelling and gesture accompany this. The games then move to joint action sequences involving turn-taking, and finally to negotiation of play in dyads and triads. As the intervention progresses, the child's role evolves from that of observer to actor to agent and finally to negotiator. The child is helped through the scaffolding of shared games by an adult to come to understand and use language meaningfully. The reported results of this intervention indicated that this approach is more successful than traditional speech therapy in developing language comprehension and use in cognitive activities.

Perhaps the best researched and most well-known programmes which aim to alter the nature of parents', carers' and educators' interaction with children, leading to improvement in the children's communication skills, are the programmes which have been developed by the Hanen centre in Canada. Currently there are five programmes with different target clients (parents of children with language delays, parents of children with autism, childhood educators, parents of children who are late talkers, parents of children who are at risk for speech and language delays). The Hanen approach derives its theoretical basis from the social interactionist perspective and, as such, views the child's active participation in frequent, reciprocal social interactions with a caregiver as the context for language learning. The programmes aim to help adults to do the following:

1 to help the child stay in the interaction or conversation so s/he can practise using communication and so s/he has opportunities to learn language in meaningful situations:
2 to provide finely tuned language models so the child can use these to progress to the next stage of communication. Research has shown that these programmes are effective in decreasing the directiveness of mothers and increasing their responsiveness. The children whose parents followed the programme demonstrated an increase in their social assertiveness and joint attention when compared with children in the control groups. They also demonstrated a more diverse, greater vocabulary and accelerated language development compared with the control group (Girolametto *et al.* 1994; Girolametto *et al.* 1996; Girolametto *et al.* 1997). One recent study reported, however, that although there was an overall change in children's social interaction skills, changes in language reception and expression were not found (Coulter and Gallagher 2001).

Clearly, in the arena of early childhood intervention there are a number of practitioners who have taken to heart the message of the social interactionists and endeavoured to implement their ideas for the benefit of children with communication difficulties. The targeting, implementation and evaluation of such programmes remain an issue, but efforts to date suggest that implementation of the suggestions of the social interactionist agenda is a key to altering dysfunctional communication between carers, educators and children.

Turning to reports of interventions at later stages of development, there are a number of interventions in the literature reported to be 'naturalistic' or 'child-centred' in their approach. A classic example of this is reported by Camarata *et al.* (1994). These authors compared conversational re-casting (a naturally occurring feature of conversations between carers and young children) and elicited imitation intervention procedures in their efficacy in promoting the use of a wide variety of syntactic structures in children aged between 4.0 and 6.10 with SLI. In conversational recasting, the mother follows the child's production with an utterance that maintains the semantic platform of the child's sentence with a production that includes some contrasts in semantic, syntactic, and/or morphological structures. These recasts have been shown to facilitate acquisition of language structures when presented to normally developing children. In the conversational procedure the clinician provided toys that were likely to elicit attempts at the target (e.g. movable figures and vehicles if the progressive 'ing' is targeted). The child and the clinician played together with the toys in naturalistic interaction. No imitative prompts or reinforcement were used. Camerata *et al.* found that the recast procedure was more effective than the imitation procedure in that fewer presentations to first spontaneous use were required and the transition to generalised spontaneous production was more rapid under the recast procedure. More spontaneous productions for the target items also occurred under the conversational training procedures. These authors suggest that 'embedding targets in ongoing conversation bypasses the inherent problems of generalisation from nonconversational contexts and reinforcers to actual conversation'. Also the conversational approach selects targets with which the child is currently challenged; incorporates the child's central semantic information from an immediately preceding utterance; and does not include requests or prompts that may disrupt the communicative context. It must be noted, however, that although this intervention used naturalistic procedures, it took place in the context of a clinic and was conducted by a clinician. Camerata *et al.* did try to establish a child-centred communicative relationship with the children, but the context and partners were not 'natural' and therefore the generalisation of the skills shown in this context is in question. Had the same intervention been used in the child's home with parental partners and relevant home activities, then this would be more in line with the premises of this approach.

Although many reported interventions advocate the use of 'naturalistic' approaches, how well is this agenda implemented in practice? Hepting and Goldstein (1996) present a useful attempt (a) to identify how and why the term 'naturalistic' is being used in the child language intervention literature; and (b) to organise the information into a framework for researchers and practitioners. In their investigation they analysed 34 'naturalistic' interventions reported in the research literature. They organised the procedures used in the interventions on a continuum ranging from most adult-centred (prompting imitation) to most child-centred (descriptive talking). Contexts (settings and trainers) were also rated on Fey's (1986) continuum of naturalness ranging from 0 (drill activities in clinics/special rooms with clinicians) to 6 (daily home activities in the child's home with parents, siblings or peers). Correlation between the rating of procedures and the rating of the naturalness of intervention context indicated that the two were quite independent of each other. Their results demonstrated that naturalistic language interventions varied considerably in the teaching techniques used. They suggest that among researchers and practitioners there is a lack of agreement on what constitutes 'naturalistic' language intervention and indeed it would seem that the 'naturalistic' aspects of some of the interventions were difficult to identify. Certainly they were unable to identify a set of common characteristics that could match with the descriptor. They found that the procedures rarely resemble the 'natural' interactions between mother and children. Hepting and Goldstein indeed suggest that the term 'naturalness' as demonstrated in these investigations is of questionable value to researchers and practitioners when the effectiveness of different intervention approaches is to be evaluated.

In a slightly later paper, Kovarsky and Duchan (1997) address an issue relating to the implementation of the social-interactionist approach by attempting to pull apart the dimensions of difference between 'adult-centred' therapy and 'child-centred' therapy. In adult-centred therapy, they suggest, the clinician talks more than the child, requests information already known to her, evades the child's efforts to initiate conversation and controls the introduction of new topics. In child-centred therapy the clinician follows the child's interactional lead and interprets behaviours as meaningful and communicative by responding in some communicative manner. As a means of differentiating the two approaches, Kovarsky and Duchan suggest five overlapping dimensions of therapy interaction, as follows:

1 *The intervention activity*: tightly scripted games/routines regulated by the adult versus open events where the child may regulate and control.
2 *The agenda*: attaining the clinician's set goals versus supporting the child's communicative goals.
3 *The lead in interaction*: adult versus child.
4 *The evaluation of the child's performance*: overt versus implicit.
5 *Repairing communication breakdowns/difficulties*: correcting errors in child's performance versus facilitating the achievement of a mutual understanding and a common code.

In their paper they give a detailed breakdown of two parts of a therapeutic interaction in which two clinicians were asked to engage specifically in child-centred therapy in turn with a 4y 7m child. The resulting analysis shows that in fact the interaction was a hybrid of adult and child-centred approaches, revealing features of both types of practice. They suggest that

> *as an interaction practice, child-centred therapy is more than simply doing away with, or changing the function of, particular communicative structures. To evaluate the child-centredness of intervention one must understand the communicative relationships between speakers as they are played out during sequences of interaction that are embedded in therapeutic events. Within a single interaction therapy may not be easily dichotomised as either adult- or child-centred.*

They suggest that in order to evaluate the child-centredness of an intervention we need to explore the type of communicative relationship the clinician seeks to foster as opposed to a set of structural properties that are either present or absent.

From these two papers it can be seen that practice in speech and language intervention is as yet a long way from adopting a whole-hearted social interactionist approach, even when the interventionist is attempting to adopt a 'naturalistic' approach. This does not mean of course that natural, child-centred intervention is impossible to achieve but rather that, given their background, training and resources, practitioners find it difficult to find ways of changing practices which match the demands of employers and clients and are also based on the ideas and skills which they have developed over time.

Radical ways forward in changing therapeutic practice are recommended in a very interesting paper addressing the importance of 'therapy in natural environments' by Hanft and Pilkington (2000). These authors take up the challenge of recent US legislation which mandates that therapeutic work should be conducted in 'settings that are natural or normal for the child's age peers who have no disabilities' (Individuals with Disabilities Education: US Code of Federal Regulations, 1997). They provide a summary of the contrasting consequences for families of the application of early intervention principles in clinic and natural settings. They suggest that therapists should explore with families how interactions and activities within familiar places can become natural contexts for learning in which the generalisation of skills is far more likely to occur. For instance, they suggest that a therapist can review with the parent which household items and toys will promote developmental skills and encourage verbal expressions. If natural contexts for learning are used, then this will help reduce the therapist's dependence on a specific place for intervention and improve the child's skills through family routines and practices.

Hanft and Pilkington provide an interesting contrast between the notions of *translating* and *transferring* professional knowledge. The latter involves telling the recipient exactly what to do in order to behave as the therapist would in a clinical setting. The former involves providing relevant information and strategies to other adults to assist them in their effort to improve a child's performance in natural settings. The therapists should vary what knowledge they share and the suggestions that they make depending on the knowledge, experience and role of the adult in question.

In conclusion, they recommend the following five guidelines for therapists:

1 Help family members articulate their priorities for a child's development by understanding how a child behaves in daily activities.
2 Prioritise meaningful functional and practical outcomes with parents to guide therapeutic objectives and intervention strategies.
3 Consider experience and support the variety of environments and adult caregivers who interact with the child in the course of a week.
4 Utilise service models with the flexibility to combine direct service with collaborative consultation with caregivers to assure generalisation of a child's new skills in daily activities.
5 Ensure ongoing, frequent evaluation of whether therapy makes a difference (i.e., moving toward achieving desired outcomes within a specified period of time).

Although their paper is aimed at all types of therapeutic practice, it seems very relevant to those working in the development of communication and language and basing their ideas on the social interactionist approach.

Given Hanft and Pilkington's agenda, two further papers on the use of naturalistic partners and settings offer some hopeful pointers to ways forward. These papers suggest that one of the key ingredients in any programme should be naturalistic communicative partners so that the difficult process of generalisation from an artificial partner to a real one can be avoided, and the communicative activities used are those that are meaningful and helpful in embedding the child within their natural cultural context.

A successful small-scale implementation of the use of peers in play to promote increased joint attention, play and language was carried out by Zercher *et al.* (2001). In this study a community setting is used which was 'naturally' occurring – a Sunday school. Two children with autism aged 6.3 were the participants, along with three normally developing children. Major play themes were identified for the non-autistic children (expert players) based on the interests of the autistic children (novice players). The non-autistic children were given specific examples of how the autistic children could be included. These were displayed on posters of 'what to do' and 'what to say'. During the sessions the observer provided direction to the non-autistic children in the form of specific prompts but she did not engage with the autistic children. As a result the expert players succeeded in creating a rich interactive situation around the novice players and the novice players became actively engaged. There were 'dramatic increases in shared attention to objects, symbolic play acts, and verbal utterances on the part of the participants with autism'. The high level and quality of the engagement were particularly noted by the parents. One parent concluded after observing a videotaped session: 'That's how normal kids play. You know? That's what we want for our boys.' Zercher *et al.* suggest that peers have a pivotal role to play in the development of social and communicative competence in children with communication disorders and in their successful integration into 'normal' school social life.

In the second paper Hadley and Schuele (1998) take up the theme of the importance of natural settings and partners. They argue that it is particularly important for speech and language therapists to target socially relevant language objectives with children with SLI because these children must live up to standard societal expectations in social, educational and vocational settings. They identify several barriers to this such as the belief that clinicians may have that the interface of language with other domains is beyond the scope of their practice; the minimal contact clinicians have with parents and teachers and the assessment methods traditionally used. They then go on to describe interventions individually designed for four different children to promote more successful social interaction. Thus Molly was assisted in increasing her initiation to peers in routine activities; David was helped to produce prosocial functional phrases and appropriate peer-directed verbal requests; Trevor was encouraged to produce initiations and responses to peers and to stay engaged in conversationally oriented dramatic play; Kurt was enabled to overcome his passivity with peers in order to achieve specific social goals such as obtaining a desired toy or entering a peer group at play.

These two papers are clearly aimed at communicative goals for children rather than at the production of correct grammatical forms and vocabulary. The premise of social interactionism is that, given the communicative motivation, form and content will follow. Correctness of form and content may, however, not be achievable until the child's metacognitive abilities can be engaged and the motivation to address such problems is established. This question of the involvement of metacognition using a social interactionist approach in therapy is addressed by Schneider and Watkins (1996). They are concerned to point out that 'limited research has specifically focussed on the application of Vygotskian principles to language intervention settings'. They contrast the concerns and procedures of standard interventions and those of the Vygotskian approach. They also consider that although clinicians often feel that they are already interacting with clients in a way that corresponds to Vygotskian scaffolding, on closer inspection, it often appears that the clinician is directing the interaction and retaining responsibility for the overall goals. They suggest that dynamic assessment (as described above) leads naturally into *dynamic intervention* which requires constant assessment of the effect of adult cues on the child's performance in order to keep the adult's assistance at the appropriate level. The goal of dynamic assessment is to determine the skills with which the child is currently ready to be helped. In dynamic intervention the goal is to assist the child to develop those skills by internalising the process carried out between the adult and the child in interaction. Schneider and Watkins provide an example of the application of this approach to enabling a 13-year-old boy with speech and language difficulties to generate and tell an original story. Here we see the utilisation with an older child of metacognitive abilities as an additional tool to enable the child gradually to develop independence in a key communicative skill.

Conclusion

To summarise, the case has been made here for the use of a social interactionist approach in assessment and intervention with children with communication difficulties. Some evidence from research and practice has been presented. It seems that much of this evidence suggests that as yet systematic, rigorous approaches to the use of social interactionist principles are few and far between, though many attempts have been made to implement these ideas. Some of the more recent approaches to work with children in the early stages of communicative development, such as those of Ward (1999), Aldred *et al.* (2001) and Smith and Fluck (2000) and the Hanen programme (Manolson 1992) seem to hold out much promise. It is to be hoped that systematic evaluation of the more widespread use of such programmes will take place. It is also to be hoped that the promotion of competent functional communication as the primary goal and the understanding of the all-importance of the nature of the partnerships will facilitate the development of practice in this area.

Cuddle and read. Using books with flaps, pop-ups, windows, etc. for agency in literacy.

Bibliography

Alderson, P. (ed.) (1999) *The Cleves School Experience: Learning and Inclusion*. London: David Fulton Publishers.

Aldred, C., Pollard, C., Phillips, R. and Adams, C. (2001) 'Multidisciplinary social communication intervention for children with autism and pervasive developmental disorder', *Educational and Child Psychology*, **18**(2), 76–87.

Andersen-Wood, L. and Smith, B.R. (1997) *Working with Pragmatics: A Practical Guide to Promoting Communicative Confidence*. Bicester: Winslow.

Arnall, D. and Webb, T. (1992) *A is for Autism*. [Video] A Finetake Production for Channel 4.

Athey, C. (1990) *Extending Thought in Young Children: A Parent/teacher Partnership*. London: Paul Chapman.

Baker, N.D. and Nelson, K.E. (1984) 'Recasting and related conversational techniques for triggering syntactic advances by young children', *First Language*, **5**, 3–22.

Barbieri, M.S. and Landolfi, L. (1994) 'Learning how to explain: the effects of mother's language on the child', in V. John-Steiner, C.P. Panofsky and L.W. Smith (eds) *Sociocultural Approaches to Language and Literacy*. Cambridge: Cambridge University Press.

Barton, L. (ed.) (1988) *The Politics of Special Educational Needs*. London: Falmer Press.

Beaver, R. (1996) *Educational Psychology Casework*. London: Jessica Kingsley.

Behar, R. (1996) *The Vulnerable Observer: Anthropology that Breaks your Heart*. Boston: Beacon Press.

Bennett, N., Wood, L. and Rogers, S. (1997) *Teaching Through Play: Teachers' Thinking and Classroom Practice*. Milton Keynes: Open University Press.

Billington, T. (2000a) *Separating, Losing and Excluding Children: Narratives of Difference*. London: Routledge.

Billington, T. (2000b) 'Autism: working with parents, and discourses in experience, expertise and learning', *Educational Psychology in Practice*, **16**(1), 59–68.

Birkeland, L. (2001) 'Story-telling and staff training in kindergarten', paper presented at EECERA Congress, Alkmaar, Holland.

Bishop D. and Adams, C. (1990) 'A prospective study of the relationship between specific language impairment, phonological disorders and reading retardation', *Journal of Child Psychology and Psychiatry*, **31**, 1027–50.

Bruner, J. (1968) *Processes of Cognitive Growth: Infancy* vol. III Heinz Warner lecture series. Worcester, MA: Clark University Press.

Bruner, J. (1980) *Under Fives in Britain*. (Oxford Research Project), Grant McIntyre.

Bruner, J. (1983) *Child Talk: Learning to Use Language*. Oxford: Oxford University Press.

Bruner, J. (1986) *Actual Minds Possible Worlds*. Cambridge, MA and London: Harvard University Press.

Bruner, J. (1996) *The Culture of Education*. New York: Harvard University Press.

Burman, E. (1994) *Deconstructing Developmental Psychology*. London and New York: Routledge.

Camarata, S.M., Nelson, K.E. and Camarata, M.N. (1994) 'Comparison of conversational recasting and imitative procedures for training grammatical structures in children with specific language impairment', *Journal of Speech and Hearing Research*, **37**, 1414–23.

Carr, M., May, H. and Podmore, V. (1998) 'Learning and teaching stories: new approaches to assessment and evaluation in relation to Te Wháriki', paper presented at symposium for the 8th European Conference on Quality in Early Childhood Settings, Santiago de Compostela, Spain.

Challoner, J. (2000) *The Brain*. London: Channel 4 Books.

Chomsky, N. (1965) *Aspects of the Theory of Syntax*. Cambridge, MA: MIT Press.

Chomsky, N. (1981) *Lectures on Government and Binding*. Dordrecht: Foris.

Clandinin, D.J. and Connolly, F.M. (1991) 'Narrative and story in practice and research', in D.A. Schön (ed.) *The Reflective Turn: Case Studies in and on Educational Practice*. New York: Teachers College Press, pp. 258–81.

Clarke, C., Dyson, A. and Milward, A. (eds) (1997) *Towards Inclusive Schools*. London: David Fulton.

Cline, T. (1992) (ed.) *The Assessment of Special Educational Needs: International Perspectives*. London: Routledge.

Clough, P. and Corbett, J. (2000) *Theories of Inclusive Education: A Students' Guide*. London: Chapman/Sage.

Cockerill, H. (n.d.) *Communication Through Play: Non-directive Communication Therapy 'Special Times'*. Cheyne Centre for Children with Cerebral Palsy. London: Blackrose Press.

Conti-Ramsden, G., Crutchley, A., Botting, N. (1997) 'The extent to which psychometric tests differentiate subgroups of children with SLI', *Journal of Speech, Language, and Hearing Research*, **40**, 765–77.

Conti-Ramsden, G. and Dykins, J. (1991) 'Mother-child interactions with language impaired children and their siblings', *British Journal of Disorders of Communication*, **26**, 333–54.

Coulter, L. and Gallagher, C. (2001) 'Evaluation of the Hanen Early Childhood Educators Programme', *International Journal of Language and Communication Disorders* **36**(2), 264–9.

Delamont, S. (1992) *Fieldwork in Educational Settings: Methods, Pitfalls, and Perspectives*. London: Falmer Press.

Dewart, H. and Summers, S. (1995) *The Pragmatics Profile of Everyday Communication Skills in Children*. Windsor: NFER-Nelson.

Dockrell, J., George, R., Lindsay, G. and Roux, J. (1997) 'Problems in the identification and assessment of children with specific speech and language disorders', *Educational Psychology in Practice*, **13**(1) April, 29–38.

Dockrell, J. and McShane, J. (1993) *Children's Learning Difficulties: A Cognitive Approach*. Oxford: Blackwell.

Dombey, H. (1993) *Reading: What Children Need to Learn and How Teachers Can Help Them*. Oxford: Blackwell.

Donaldson, M. (1978) *Children's Minds*. London: Collins.

Duffy, B. (1998) 'Talking with and listening to young children', in S. Smidt (ed.) *The Early Years: A Reader*. London: Routledge.

Edwards, C., Gandini, L. and Forman, G. (eds) (1998) *The Hundred Languages of Children: The Reggio Emilia Approach – Advanced Reflections*. London: JAI Press Ltd.

Eisner, E. (1993) 'Objectivity in educational research', in M. Hammersley (ed.) *Educational Research and Current Issues*, vol. I, London: Paul Chapman.

Ekiksen Ødegaard, E. (2001) 'Prospects and dilemmas in kindergarten stories', paper presented at EECERA Congress, Alkmaar, Holland.

Ellis Weismer, S. (2000) 'Intervention for children with developmental language delay', in D. Bishop and L. Leonard (eds) *Speech and Language Impairments in Children: Causes, Characteristics, Intervention and Outcome*. Hove: Psychology Press, pp. 157–78.

Faupel, A., Herrick, E. and Sharp, P. (1998) *Anger Management*. London: David Fulton.

Feuerstein, R., Rand, Y. and Hoffman, M.B. (1979) *The Dynamic Assessment of Retarded Performers. The L.P.A.D. Theory, Instruments and Techniques*. Glenview, IL: Scott Foresman Press.

Fey, M. (1986) *Language Intervention with Young Children*. San Diego, CA: College-Hill Press.

Fisher, J. (1996) *Starting from the Child? Teaching and Learning from 4–8*. Buckingham: Open University Press.

Frith, U. (1990) *Autism: Explaining the Enigma*. Oxford: Blackwell.

Gallaway, C. and Richards, B.J. (1994) *Input and Interaction in Language Acquisition*. Cambridge: Cambridge University Press.

Garton, A.F. (1992) *Social Interaction and the Development of Language and Cognition*. London: Erlbaum.

Girolametto, L.E., Pearce, P. and Weitzman, E. (1996) 'Interactive focused stimulation for toddlers with expressive vocabulary delays', *Journal of Speech and Hearing Research* **39**, 1274–83.

Girolametto, L., Pearce, P. and Weitzman, E. (1997) 'The effects of lexical intervention on the phonology of late talkers', *Journal of Speech, Language and Hearing Research* **40**, 338–48.

Girolametto, L.E., Verbey, M. and Tannock, R. (1994) 'Improving joint engagement in parent-child interaction: an intervention study', *Journal of Early Intervention* **18**(2), 155–67.

Glogowska, M., Roulstone, S., Enderby, P. and Peters, T.J. (2000) 'Randomised controlled trial of community based speech and language therapy in preschool children', *British Medical Journal* **321**, 923–6.

Gopnik, A., Meltsoff, A. and Kuhl, P. (1999) *How Babies Think*. London: Weidenfeld and Nicolson.

Goswami, U. and Bryant, P. (1990) *Phonological Skills and Learning to Read*. London: Lawrence Erlbaum.

Gray, D.E. and Denicolo, P. (1998) 'Research in special needs education: objectivity or ideology?', *British Journal of Special Education*, **25**, 140–5.

Greenhough, P. and Hughes, M. (1998) 'Parents' and teachers' interventions in children's reading', *British Educational Research Journal*, **24**(4), 383–98.

Griffiths, F. (2000) 'Play Partners: parental involvement in a pre-school project for children with communication difficulties', in S. Wolfendale (ed.) *Special Needs in the Early Years: Snapshots of Practice*. London: Routledge.

Hadley, P.A. and Schuele, C.M. (1998) 'Facilitating peer interaction: socially relevant objectives for preschool language intervention', *American Journal of Speech-Language Pathology* **7**, 25–36.

Hamill, D. and Larson, S. (1974) 'The relationship of selected auditory perceptual skills and reading ability', *Journal of Learning Disabilities* **7**, 429–35.

Hammersley, M. (ed.) (1993) *Educational Research and Current Issues*. London: Paul Chapman.

Hanft, B.E. and Pilkington, K.O. (2000) 'Therapy in natural environments: the means or end goal for early intervention?', *Infants and Young Children* **12**(4), 1–13.

Hanko, G. (1999) *Increasing Competence through Collaborative Problem-Solving Using Insight into Social and Emotional Factors in Children's Learning*. London: David Fulton.

Harris, M. (1992) *Language Experience and Early Language Development: From Input to Uptake*. London: Erlbaum.

Hart, B. (2000) 'A natural history of early language experience: topics in early childhood', *Special Education* **20**(1), 28–32.

Hatch, A. and Wisniewski, R. (eds) (1995) *Life History and Narrative*. London: Falmer Press.

Hepting, N.H. and Goldstein, H. (1996) 'What's natural about naturalistic language intervention?', *Journal of Early Intervention* **20**(3), 249–65.

Hohmann, M. (1979) *Young Children in Action: The Cognitively Orientated Preschool Curriculum: A Manual for Preschool Educators*. Ypselanti, MI: High Scope Press.

Hollway, W. and Jefferson, T. (2000) *Doing Qualitative Research Differently: Free Association, Narrative and the Interview Method*. London: Sage.

Holly, M.L. (1989) 'Reflective writing and the spirit of enquiry', *Cambridge Journal of Education* **19**(1), 71–80.

Holquist, M. (1990) *Bakhtin and His World*. London: Routledge.

Johnson-Laird, P.N. (1983) *Mental Models: Towards a Cognitive Science of Language, Inference and Consciousness*. Cambridge, MA: Harvard University Press.

Karmiloff-Smith, A. (1994) *Baby, It's You*. London: Ebury Press.

Katz, L. (1995) 'The professional pre-school teacher', in L. Katz (ed.) *Talks with Teachers of Young Children*. New Jersey: Ablex.

Kerbel, D. and Grunwell, P. (1998) 'A play-based methodology for assessing comprehension in children with semantic-pragmatic difficulties', *European Journal of Disorders of Communication* **31**, 65–75.

Kersner, M. and Wright, J. (1993) *How to Manage Communication Problems in Young Children*. Bicester: Winslow Press.

Kovarsky, D. and Duchan, J.F. (1997) 'The interactional dimensions of language therapy', *Language, Speech and Hearing Services in Schools* **28**, 297–307.

Lakoff, G. and Johnson, M. (1980) *Metaphors We Live By*. London: University of Chicago Press.

Law, J. and Conti-Ramsden, G. (2000) 'Treating children with speech and language impairments', *British Medical Journal* **321**, 908–9.

Leinonen, E., Letts, C. and Smith, B.R. (2000) *Children's Pragmatic Communication Difficulties*. London: Whurr.

Lewis, A. and Norwich, B. (1999) *Mapping a Pedagogy for Special Educational Needs*. BERA monograph. Exeter University: School of Education.

Liddle, S. (1999) 'An evaluation through observation of pre-school children with language and communication impairment in their integrated mainstream nursery and a segregated setting', MPhil thesis under revision from the University of Newcastle upon Tyne Speech Sciences.

Lidz, C.S. (1991) *Practitioner's Guide to Dynamic Assessment*. New York: Guilford Press.

Linder, T.W. (1993) *Transdisciplinary Play-based Assessment: A Functional Approach to Working with Young Children*. Baltimore: Paul Brookes Publishing Co.

Lord, C., Rutter, M., Goode, S., Heemsbergen, J., Jordan, H., Mawhood, L. and Schopler (1989) 'Autism diagnostic observation schedule', *Journal of Autism and Developmental Disorders* **20**, 115–29.

MacGrath, M. (1988) *The Art of Teaching Peacefully*. London: David Fulton.

Mackay, M. and Watson, J. (1989) 'Games for promoting communication', *British Journal of Special Education* **16**, 58–61.

Macmillan, B. (1997) *Why Schoolchildren Can't Read*. London: IEA Studies in Education and Training Unit.

Manolson, A. (1992) *It Takes Two to Talk: A Parent's Guide to Helping Children Communicate*. Available from The Hanen Centre, Suite 3–390, 252 Bloor St. West, Toronto, ON M5S 1V6.

Marshall, J.C. (1981) 'Hemispheric specialisation – what, how and why', *Behavioural and Brain Sciences* **4**(1), 72–3.

Martin, T. (1989) *The Strugglers*. Milton Keynes: Open University Press.

McGuinness, D. (1988) *Why Children Can't Read and What We Can Do About It*. London: Penguin.

Mearig, J.S. (1987) 'Assessing the learning potential of kindergarten and primary aged children', in C.S. Lidz (ed.) *Dynamic Assessment: An Interactional Approach to Evaluating Learning Potential*. New York: Guilford Press.

Mellor, N. (1997) *Attention Seeking: A Practical Solution for the Classroom*. Bristol: Lucky Duck.

Mellor, N. (1999) *The Good, the Bad and the Irritating*. Bristol: Lucky Duck.

Mellor, N. (n.d.) *Cuddle and Read*. North Shields: North Tyneside M.B.C.

Mortimore, P. (ed.) (1999) *Understanding Pedagogy and Its Impact on Learning*. London: Sage.

Nelson, K.E. (1977) 'Facilitating children's syntax acquisition', *Developmental Psychology* **13**, 101–7.

Nelson, K.E. (1985) *Event Representation and Cognitive Development.* Chicago: Lawrence Erlbaum.

Nelson, K.E., Camarata, S.M., Welsh, J., Butkovsky, L. and Camarata, M. (1996) 'Effects of imitative and conversational recasting treatment on the acquisition of grammar in children with specific language impairment and younger language normal children', *Journal of Speech and Hearing Research* **39**(4), 850–9.

Nelson, N.W. (1993) *Childhood Language Disorders in Context: Infancy Through Adolescence.* New York: Macmillan.

Newman, T. (1999) *Evidence-based Child Care Practice.* Highlight no. 170. London: National Children's Bureau.

Nind, M. and Hewitt, D. (1996) *Access to Communication: Developing the Basics of Communication with People with Severe Learning Difficulties through Intensive Interaction.* London: David Fulton.

Novak, M. (1975) 'Story and experience', in J.B. Wiggins (ed.) *Religion as Story.* Lanham, MD: University Press of America, pp. 175–200.

Nutbrown, C. (1994) *Threads of Thinking: Young Children Learning and the Role of Early Education.* London: Paul Chapman.

Oliver, M. (1996) *Understanding Disability: From Theory to Practice.* Basingstoke: Macmillan.

Ortony, A. (ed.) (1993) *Metaphor and Thought.* Cambridge: Cambridge University Press.

Parelli, P. (1993) *Natural Horsemanship.* Colorado Springs: Western Horseman Inc.

Parlett, M. (1991) 'The assessment of hearing-impaired children', in D. Schön (ed.) *The Reflective Turn: Case Studies in and on Educational Practice.* New York and London: Teachers College Press, pp. 213–32.

Pellegrini, A.D. (2001) 'Practitioner review: the role of direct observation in the assessment of young children', *Journal of Child Psychology and Psychiatry* **42**(7), 861–9.

Pellegrini, A.D. and Galda, L. (1998) *The Development of School-based Literacy: A Social Ecological Study.* London: Routledge.

Piaget, J. (1926) *The Language and Thought of the Child.* London: Routledge & Kegan Paul.

Piaget, J. (1954) *The Construction of Reality in the Child.* New York: Basic Books Inc.

Pijl, S.J., Meijer, C.J.W. and Hegarty, S. (eds) (1997) 'Inclusion: implementation and approaches', in S.J. Pijl, C.J.W. Meijer and S. Hegarty (eds) *Inclusive Education: A Global Agenda.* London: Routledge.

Pinker, S. (1987) 'The boot-strapping problem in language acquisition', in B. Macwhinney (ed.) *Mechanisms of Language Acquisition.* Hillsdale, NJ: Lawrence Erlbaum.

Polanyi, M. (1967) *The Tacit Dimension.* London: Routledge and Kegan Paul.

Pontecorvo, C. (1998) 'Changing the metaphors of childhood learning: from interiorisation to participation', keynote lecture at 8th European Conference on Quality in Early Childhood Settings, Santiago de Compostela, Spain.

Pourde, L. (1989) *Classroom Listening and Speaking.* Tucson, AZ: Communication Skill Builders.

Pratt, M.W., Kerig, P., Cowan, P.A. and Cowan, C.P. (1988) 'Mothers and fathers teaching three-year-olds: authoritative parenting and adult scaffolding of young children's learning', *Developmental Psychology* **24**, 832–9.

Quick, J. and O'Neal, A. (1997) *Promoting Communication.* Vero Beach, FL: The Speech Bin.

Reggio Children (1997) *The Hundred Languages of Children.* Reggio Emilia, Italy. Published by Reggio Children.

Richer, J. and Coates, S. (eds) (2001) *Autism: A Search for Coherence.* London: Jessica Kingsley.

Rickerby, S. and Lambert, S. (1997) *Listening Skills.* Birmingham: The Questions Publishing Co.

Riddick, B. (2000) 'An examination of the relationship between labelling and stigmatisation with special reference to dyslexia', *Disability and Society* **15**(4), 653–67.

Rispens, J. and van Yperen, T.A. (1997) 'How specific are specific developmental disorders?', *Journal of Psychology and Child Psychiatry* **38**(3), 351–63.

Roberts, M. (1997) *The Man Who Listens to Horses.* UK: Arrow Books.

Rodger, R. (1994) 'A quality curriculum for the early years: raising some questions', in L. Abbott and R. Rodger (eds) *Quality Education in the Early Years.* Buckingham: Open University Press.

Rogers, C.R. (1961) *On Becoming a Person.* Boston, MA: Houghton Mifflin.

Rosen, M. (1993) *We're Going on a Bear Hunt.* London: Walker Books.

Rouse, M. and Florian, L. (1996) 'Effective inclusive schools: a study in two countries', *Cambridge Journal of Education* **26**, 1.

Schaffer, H.R. (1996) *Social Development.* Oxford: Blackwell.

Scherer, N. and Olswang, L. (1984) 'Role of mothers' expansions in children's language production', *Journal of Speech and Hearing Research* **27**, 387–96.

Schneider, P. and Watkins, R.V. (1996) 'Applying Vygotskian developmental theory to language intervention', *Language, Speech and Hearing Services in Schools* **27**, 157–69.

Schön, D.A. (1983) *The Reflective Practitioner: How Professionals Think in Action.* Aldershot: Avebury.

Schön, D.A. (1997) *Educating the Reflective Practitioner.* San Francisco: Jossey-Bass Publishers.

Sebba, J. and Ainscow, M. (1996) 'International developments in inclusive schooling: mapping the issues', *Cambridge Journal of Education* **26**(1), 5–18.

Shapiro, T., Frosch, E. and Arnold, S. (1987) 'Communicative interaction between mothers and their autistic children: application of a new instrument and changes after treatment', *Journal of the American Academy of Child and Adolescent Psychiatry* **26**, 485–90.

Sharp, P. (2001) *Nurturing Emotional Intelligence: A Practical Guide for Teachers, Parents and Those in the Caring Professions.* London: David Fulton.

Sher, B. (1995) *Popular Games for Positive Play.* Tucson, AZ: Therapy Skill Builders.

Singer, J.L. (1973) *The Child's World of Make-believe.* New York: Academic Press.

Skinner, B.F. (1957) *Verbal Behaviour.* Norwalk, CT: Appleton-Century-Crofts.

Smith, C. (1995) 'A developmental approach to pre-linguistic intervention', paper for Educational Psychologists' Interest Group (Gateshead Teachers' Centre) when in preparation for a doctoral thesis from Portsmouth University.

Smith, C. and Fluck, M. (2000) 'Re-constructing pre-linguistic interpersonal processes to promote language development in young children with deviant or delayed communication skills', *British Journal of Educational Psychology* **70**(3), 369–89.

Smith, C. and Fluck, M. (2001) *Scheme to Promote Early Interactive Conversations.* Portsmouth: University of Portsmouth Publications.

Snowling, M.J. (2000) 'Language and literacy skills: who is at risk and why?', in D. Bishop and L. Leonard (eds) *Speech and Language Impairments in Children: Causes, Characteristics, Intervention and Outcome.* Hove: Psychology Press.

Snowling, M.J., Nation, K and Muter, V. (1999) 'The role of semantic and phonological skills in learning to read: implications for assessment and teaching', in T. Nunes (ed.) *Learning to Read: An Integrated View from Research and Practice.* Dordrecht: Kluwer, pp. 195–208.

Stackhouse, J. (2000) 'Barriers to literacy development in children with speech and language difficulties', in D. Bishop and L. Leonard (eds) *Speech and Language Impairments in Children: Causes, Characteristics, Intervention and Outcome.* Hove: Psychology Press, pp. 73–98.

Swann, W. (1988) 'Trends in special school placement to 1986: measuring, assessing and explaining segregation', *Oxford Review of Education* **14**(2), 139–61.

Sylva, K., Roy, C. and Painter, M. (1980) *Childwatching at Playgroup and Nursery School.* Grant McIntyre Ltd.

Thomas, G. (1997) 'Inclusive schools for an inclusive society', *British Journal of Special Education* **24**(3), 103–7.

Tinbergen, E.A. and Tinbergen, N. (1972) 'Early childhood autism: an ethological approach', *Advances in Ethology,* **10.**

Tizard, B. and Hughes, M. (1984) *Young Children Learning: Talking and Thinking at Home and at School.* London: Collins.

Tomasello, M. and Farrar, M. (1986) 'Joint attention and early language', *Child Development* **57**, 1454–63.

Topping, K. (1988) *Paired Reading Training Pack.* Huddersfield: Kirklees Psychological.

Topping, K. (1995) *Paired Reading, Spelling and Writing.* London: Cassell.

Topping, K. and Lindsay, G.A. (1992) 'Paired reading: a review of the literature', *Research Papers in Education* **7**(3), 199–246.

Tough, J. (1977) *Talking and Learning: A Guide to Fostering Communication Skills in Nursery and Infant Schools.* London: School Council Publications: Ward Lock Educational/ Drake Educational Associates.

Trevarthen, C. (1979) 'Communication and co-operation in early infancy: a description of primary inter-subjectivity', in M. Bullowa (ed.) *Before Speech: The Beginnings of Human Communication.* Cambridge: Cambridge University Press.

Trevarthen, C. and Aitken, K.J. (2001) 'Infant intersubjectivity', *Journal of Child Psychology and Psychiatry and Allied Disciplines* **42**(1), 3–48.

Tripp, D. (1993) *Critical Incidents in Teaching.* London: Routledge.

Van de Lely, H.K.J. (1993) 'Specific language impairment in children: research findings and their therapeutic implications', *European Journal of Disorders of Communication* **28**, 247–61.

Vedeler, L. (1996) 'Pragmatic difficulties and socio-emotional problems: a case study', *European Journal of Disorders of Communication* **31**, 271–88.

Vygotsky, L.S. (1962) *Thought and Language*. Cambridge, MA: MIT Press.

Vygotsky, L.S. (1978) *Mind in Society: The Development of Higher Psychological Processes*. Cambridge, MA: Harvard University Press.

Ward, S. (1999) 'An investigation into the effectiveness of an early intervention method for delayed language development in young children', *International Journal of Language and Communication Disorders* **34**(3), 243–64.

Warren, S.F. (2000) 'The future of early communication and language intervention', *Topics in Early Childhood Special Education* **20**(1), 33–7.

Waters, J. (1999) *Let's Play: A Guide to Interactive Assessment with Young Children*. Newcastle upon Tyne: Newcastle upon Tyne LEA.

Waters, J. and Stringer, P. (1998) 'The Bunny Bag: a dynamic approach to the assessment of preschool children', *Educational and Child Psychology* **14**(4), 95–105.

Weber, S.G. (1993) *Sequences Galore*. Greenville, SC: Super Duper publications.

Webster, A. (1987) 'Enabling language acquisition: the developmental evidence', *British Psychological Society: Division of Educational and Child Psychology Newsletter*, **27**, 25–31.

Webster, A. (1992) 'Images of deaf children as learners: the influence of adults' perceptions on assessment and intervention', in T. Cline (ed.) *The Assessment of Special Educational Needs: International Perspectives*. London: Routledge.

Weitzman, E. (1992) *Learning Language and Loving It*. Toronto: Hanen Publications.

Wells, G. (1981) *Learning Through Interaction: The Study of Language Development*. Cambridge: Cambridge University Press.

Wells, G. (1987) *The Meaning Makers: Children Learning Language*. London: Hodder and Stoughton.

Wilcox, A. and Mogford-Bevan, K. (1995) 'Conversational disability: assessment and remediation', in M. Perkins and S. Howard (eds) *Case Studies in Clinical Linguistics*. London: Whurr, pp. 146–78.

Williams, D. (1996) *Autism: An Inside-out Approach*. London: Doubleday.

Wittmann, S. (1998) 'In vivo versus in vitro: "in the clinic I can do it but see me in the classroom or playground and I can't" – using formal and informal language assessments with speech and language impaired children', *Child Language and Therapy* **14**, 135–50.

Wold, A.H. (ed.) (1992) *The Dialogical Alternative: Towards a Theory of Language and Mind*. Bergen: Scandinavian University Press distributed by Oxford University Press.

Wolfberg, P.J. (1999) *Play and Imagination in Children with Autism*. New York and London: Teachers College Press.

Wood, H. and Wood, D. (1988) 'Questioning the preschool child', in A. Cohen and L. Cohen (eds) *Early Education: The Preschool Years*, PCP.

Yoder, P.J., Warren, S.F., McCathren, R.B. and Leew, S. (1998) 'Does adult responsivity to child behaviour facilitate communication development?', in A.M. Wetherby, S.F. Warren and J. Reichle (eds) *Transitions in Prelinguistic Communication*. Baltimore: Brookes.

Zerchner, C., Hunt, P., Schuler, A. and Webster, J. (2001) 'Increasing joint attention, play and language through peer supported play', *Autism* **5**(4), 374–98.

Index